Movement Study
and
Benesh Movement Notation

*An introduction to applications in
dance, medicine, anthropology, and other studies*

Julia McGuinness-Scott

Notation illustrations by
Cristiana Sequeira

London
OXFORD UNIVERSITY PRESS
New York   Melbourne
1983

Oxford University Press, Walton Street, Oxford OX2 6DP

LONDON   GLASGOW   NEW YORK   TORONTO
DELHI   BOMBAY   CALCUTTA   MADRAS   KARACHI
KUALA LUMPUR   SINGAPORE   HONG KONG   TOKYO
NAIROBI   DAR ES SALAAM   CAPE TOWN
MELBOURNE   AUCKLAND

and associate companies in

BEIRUT   BERLIN   IBADAN   MEXICO CITY

First published 1983

ISBN 0 19 317106 6

British Library Cataloguing in Publication Data

McGuinness-Scott, Julia
   Movement study and Benesh movement
   notation.
   1. Dance notation
   I. Title
   793.3'2   GV1587
   ISBN 0-19-317106-6

Typeset by Keyset Composition, Colchester, Essex
Printed in Great Britain by
Halstan & Co. Ltd., Amersham, Bucks.

Forewords

Sir Frederick Ashton

I welcome Julia McGuinness-Scott's book, attempting as it does to give a comprehensive survey of the way Benesh notation works, and the startling progress it has already made since Rudolf Benesh first presented the dance world with his ingenious invention in 1956.

Few people would expect to study music, much less be proficient in it, without the use of a music notation, and slowly and painfully we seem to be edging towards the same happy situation in dance. I know from my own experience what a difference the notation has made in the staging of my ballets in faraway places, often just a matter of company notators exchanging scores just as they do in the world of music. At the same time we must not claim too much for notation, and I am glad to see that Julia McGuinness-Scott is clear about its limitations as well as its virtues. Just as a music score needs a conductor and an orchestra to interpret it afresh, so the intangibles of style, of phrasing, of emphasis and all the subtleties of actual performance remain among the secrets of art, secrets often shared only by choreographers and performers.

That said, it is hardly possible to overstate the advantages the notation has brought to dance, now happily losing its former status as a neglected Cinderella among the other arts, now that we have acquired a language of movement that can be written down simply and read easily, so that our 'mute' art has become literate and academically respectable at last.

Helen W. Atkinson

School of Physiotherapy
Coventry (Lanchester) Polytechnic

The harmonious coordination of the human locomotor system, giving smooth production of complex and variable patterns of activity, monitored and adjusted to suit the changing needs of the individual, is an essential to the development of the whole person. Under normal circumstances this harmony develops naturally during the maturation process of the individual who spends little time thinking about how a skill is achieved, his only concern being that it has fulfilled his objective to his satisfaction.

However, those who work in situations where quality of movement is important for whatever reason (dancers, dramatic artists, sportsmen and women, gymnasts, ergonomists, physiotherapists, paediatricians and other medical personnel), need to study more deeply the complexities of human movement activities, including the relevant, sub-conscious postural adjustments which are so essential to successful application of skills and so commonly overlooked.

Such study demands careful observation of movement and meticulous analysis of its components so that, if any adjustment is needed to produce a more appropriate effect, it is carefully constructed to produce success. If the study of movement in these important fields is successful, the result, in dancing and dramatic art, is a more pleasing and interpretive performance; in sport and gymnastics, a greater measure of success; in industry, an improvement in efficiency and reduction of industrial injuries and, in the medical world, a return towards normality in patients with movement difficulties.

An ability to record the observations made, so that accurate evidence of the analysis is available, has been sought over the years, and workers in the different fields have produced their own methods with varying levels of success. The use of words is tedious and time-consuming and even the use of verbal shorthand, such as that used by physiotherapists, is unsuccessful, in that it does not fully depict the analysis, can cope with very limited variations and does not permit recording of quality and timing. In fact, its limitations have created a situation where it has now largely fallen into disuse and has not been replaced by any other method.

Such workers in the medical field and in many other disciplines have resorted to the use of more complex and expensive methods of recording and analysing movement, involving photography, video equipment and the use of computer systems. Whilst these are of great value in the well-equipped unit or studio they do not cater so readily for 'field work' and general use on the 'shop floor'. Additionally, they do not educate the worker to observe very carefully because the equipment will do it for them. Furthermore, distortion can occur in photography due to lighting and lack of the third dimension.

Dancers and gymnasts use all the above methods but have also developed the use of notation of various kinds, of which Benesh Movement Notation and Labanotation are probably the most well known and most commonly used.

In this book on Movement Study and Benesh Movement Notation, the notation has been introduced as a method of analysis as well as a recording system. The method demonstrates how the notation may be used to enable the observer to accurately analyse what is seen and record it in a relatively visual manner so that the skilled reader can not only understand what has occurred, but can also reproduce the activities with accuracy and precision; the only apparatus required being a sharp pencil, a rubber and a sheet of manuscript paper. A high level of accuracy can be reached, including the analysis and recording of the subtle postural reactions mentioned earlier and the precise movements of fingers and hand in skilled activities.

The book then continues to show the use of Benesh Movement Notation in different 'movement languages' relevant to specific fields, giving a history of its development and, finally, offers a useful further reading list to assist the student in a more comprehensive study of the subject. It should be understood that the ability to notate cannot be achieved by reading alone. A comprehensive study requires the integration of theory with practical application under the supervision of an experienced notator. In some fields of work, such as physiotherapy, ergonometry, dance and gymnastics, there is great value in the development of notation skills in the basic education of the individual worker.

After conducting short Introductory Courses in clinical recording with my own students in the School of Physiotherapy the value of the notation has become very apparent as an adjunct to the development of observational powers and the students' appreciation of movement as a whole.

John Blacking

Professor of Social Anthropology
The Queen's University of Belfast

Since Arnold Haskell wrote the foreword to Rudolf and Joan Benesh's *An Introduction to Benesh Dance Notation* (A. and C. Black, 1956), Benesh notation has become a household word in the world of professional dance; several groups of students have been trained at the Institute of Choreology and worked in a variety of fields; and many dance companies employ notators to ensure that choreography is recorded and can be more easily transmitted and learnt on subsequent occasions.

Notation gives to dance a degree of permanence, and allows works to be studied reflectively and critically away from the excitement of performance. It holds out possibilities for a new kind of dance creation, though I do not know of any major choreographer who has yet composed exclusively in notation before working with dancers. It differs from video and film records of dance, in that it incorporates the subjective elements of the choreographer's intentions and the notator's perceptions and understandings of them.

Notation is in itself a kind of pre-analysis of dance, whose practice sharpens the user's observations. One trained dancer notator was able to identify from films the crucial elements of movement in an entirely unfamiliar idiom, the dances of an African society, note them and learn them from the notation, and then perform them to the satisfaction of critical members of that society. Though trained dancers were, on another occasion, better at learning African dances than the untrained, it seemed that a dancer who could also do notation was better at grasping the essentials of a new style and performing it satisfactorily. Thus, though many fine dancers have no difficulty in learning unfamiliar styles quickly and accurately, it seems likely that the study of notation would be a useful addition to any dancer's training.

There are, of course, many other kinds of notation, of which Labanotation is perhaps the best known and the most widely used. Benesh notation is interestingly different, in that it can be neatly combined with music notation and its essentially visual characteristics make it particularly appropriate for theatre dance. It was for this art that it was originally invented by the late Rudolf Benesh, who was a painter, in collaboration with his wife Joan, who was a dancer. It is a measure of his remarkable

achievement that his system has become so well established, firmly insti-
tutionalized, and widely used.

The main difference between the 1956 introduction and Julia
McGuinness-Scott's book is that a notation specifically designed for
dance has successfully been converted into a flexible tool for noting
movement in general. The author describes many of the different ways in
which the original notation has been expanded and applied, especially in
medicine and industry. To become a proficient Benesh dance notator
takes at least a year of intensive training and to become a proficient
Benesh clinical notator takes three months. Changes in patterns of
movement can be important signs of health or disease, and of successful
or unsuccessful adaptations to work routines.

Perhaps there will be a time when every large factory and hospital, as
well as every dance company, will have a fulltime professional notator.
Whatever the future brings, Julia McGuinness-Scott's book is most
welcome as an introduction to Benesh Movement Notation for workers in
a variety of fields where human movement is a focus of study or aesthetic
pleasure.

Acknowledgements

Extract from 'La Fille mal gardée' reproduced by kind permission of Sir Frederick Ashton and The Royal Opera House, Covent Garden
Choreography © Frederick Ashton, London 1960

The 'British Sign Language' examples are from 'The Line Drawing Illustrations for the Revised Makaton Vocabulary' third edition, August 1980. My thanks to Margaret Walker, Project Co-ordinator, Makaton Vocabulary Development Project, for her assistance

Extract from Act III of 'Anastasia' reproduced by kind permission of Kenneth MacMillan. Choreography © Kenneth MacMillan, Berlin 1967

Extract from '5 Tango's' reproduced by kind permission of Hans van Manen. Choreography © Hans van Manen, Amsterdam 1977

Extract from 'Step at a Time' reproduced by kind permission of Siobhan Davies and London Contemporary Dance Trust Ltd. Choreography © Siobhan Davies, London 1976

Preface

Human movement is a complex but fascinating subject, the study and recording of it demanding a combination of many skills. This book aims to introduce all students of human movement to Benesh Movement Notation (BMN) and demonstrate its application in a number of fields of movement study. Part I describes the fundamentals of BMN. A logical method of analysing (dissecting) posture and movement is presented parallel to the explanation of the Notation. Part II describes its application in specific fields of movement which are known as movement languages. The movement languages described represent the current state of BMN usage.* Additionally, in Part II further Notation is introduced where it has particular relevance to the type of movement discussed. However, these additional topics can be equally applied to all movement.

Different forms of communication are perceived through highly evolved sense organs. For example speech, which is perceived through the ears, has a phonetically based construction, therefore the notation of speech – writing – is phonetic in structure. Music is also perceived through the ears but relates time, pitch, and volume. Its notation is therefore based on interval duration and modulation. Movement is perceived through the eyes. Consequently, a movement notation should be visually based and conform to the manner in which a kinaesthetic image of the human body, observed consciously by a trained person and subconsciously by an untrained person, is gained. The notation will therefore be logical, efficient, and practical when based on a model structured on visual perception.[1] Because we all perceive movement visually we are already trained in everyday life to read movement provided it is presented in a visual manner. Just as a reader does not see letters on the page and 'translate' them into words of a language, the reader of BMN does not see

---

* BMN has only recently entered fields such as behavioural psychology, gymnastics, theatre and television directing, and computers. As background material is not yet freely available, they have not been included in this volume.

1 *Benesh Movement Notation*, R. Benesh, *Quest* Monograph XXIII (January 1975).

the Notation signs in isolation, but reads them directly as movement patterns.

The practicality of a notation system can be measured and its efficiency judged by its ability to describe all movement, both gross and fine, in any given movement field. It must record the three dimensions of space and the dimension of time. The system must be neutral to all theories of movement so that the recording is an accurate description of the movements. By NOT classifying movement recordings it then becomes possible to apply any theory of analysis to the data.

For accurate perception of the notation signs they should be kept to a minimum and be simple in shape. The simpler the signs, the more likely it is that they will be accurately perceived. The signs should be consistent in size and proportion to facilitate speedy recognition. The basic sign shapes should be few and simple so that they can be logically and consistently developed to give rise to a vast notation vocabulary. They should be as symmetrical as possible so that by manipulation in an asymmetrical manner they carry additional information.

For reading efficiency the shape of the notation should conform to the movements of the hand and eye with which we are already familiar, our eyes, for example, being trained to scan a page from left to right. This manner of writing movement notation also enables other notations such as music and mathematics to be easily integrated with it.

Written, musical, and mathematical notations have been tools of creative thought for centuries. Mathematical notations made possible the great strides in science and technology, and the rapid development of computer sciences could not have occurred without the invention of symbolic logic and associated notations. It therefore seems quite probable that movement notation, though created so late in the day, as it were, will take its natural place alongside the others. As an increasing number of technologists, clinicians, researchers, and artists become literate in the study of movement, rapid developments will occur; some along existing lines, others no doubt in directions at present unimagined. The scope and potential of the scientific and aesthetic study of human movement has been immeasurably increased through the application of Benesh Movement Notation.[1]

1   'An Alphabet of Movement', F. Hall, *New Scientist* (October 1965).

Contents

Part One
The Notation

1. *How the Notation Works*

The Stave

The Notation is written on a five-lined stave which forms an ergonomically suitable matrix for the human body, whether the movements to be notated are running, rolling, falling through the air, dancing, walking or any other form of movement. It always records the person from behind. This way of viewing and recording enables the reader to identify his own body image on the recorded information, and ensures easy identification of right and left limb and torso movements.

With arms extended sideways at the shoulders the arm span equals the height of the body, thus forming a square. This square is imagined on the Notation stave and it is within this frame that posture and movement are recorded. Fig. 1 illustrates the anatomical points at which the five stave lines intersect the body. These points of intersection remain constant in all postures and movements.

Fig. 1

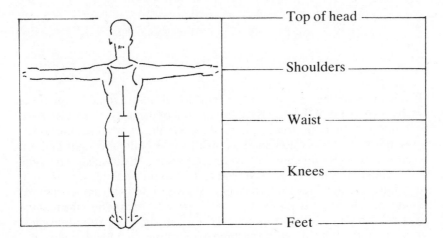

Notating extremities

The extremities (in this case understood to be the hands and feet) are related to the body in the following three ways:

1   *level* with the body.
2   *in front* of the body.
3   *behind* the body.

Three basic signs denote these relationships:

1   level   —

2   in front |

3   behind   ●

'Level' can be easily visualized as the area surrounding the body if one were to stand within the archway of a wall, the depth of the wall being equal to the thickness of the body. When the arms or legs are placed anywhere within the archway they are 'level with the body'.

Fig. 2

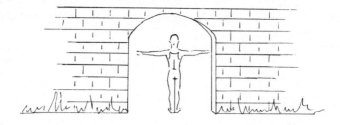

If the arms or legs move to a position where they extend through the archway in front of the wall they are 'in front of the body'. Likewise when extended through the archway behind the wall they are 'behind the body'.

A body midline is imagined as dividing the body into right and left sections. It is also imagined as dividing the frame on the stave. The three basic signs, plotted on the stave and related to the midline, are sufficient to notate an unambiguous record of the upright body with limbs extended in space. When an extremity sign is written on the right side of the midline it is plotting a right hand or foot. Likewise, when an extremity sign is written on the left side of the midline it is plotting a left hand or foot.

Fig. 3

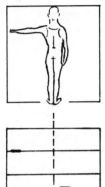

Fig. 4

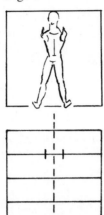

Fig. 5

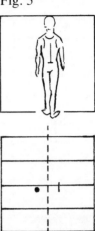

Standing on two feet

Fig. 6

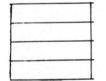

The feet are level and touching each other. When the sign is written under the bottom line, the feet are flat on the ground.

N.B. As the feet are touching the two level signs are joined.

Fig. 7

The feet are level, touching each other. The sign is written through the bottom line, denoting that only the balls of the feet are touching the ground.

Fig. 8

The feet are level, touching each other. The sign is written on top of the line, denoting that only the tips of the toes are touching the ground.

Fig. 9

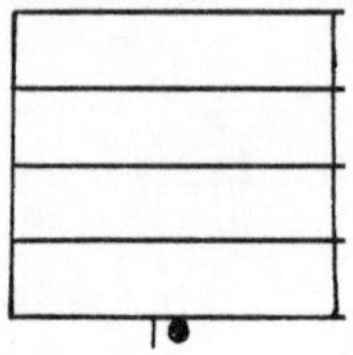

Left foot in front of body, right foot behind body, both flat on the ground (the centre of gravity is *between* the feet).

Fig. 10

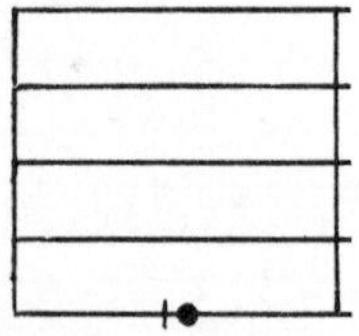

The same position as Fig. 9, but with the heels off the ground.

Standing on one foot

Fig. 11

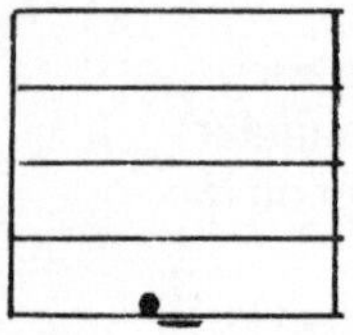

Standing on right foot, the left leg extended behind the body with only the toes touching the ground.

Fig. 12

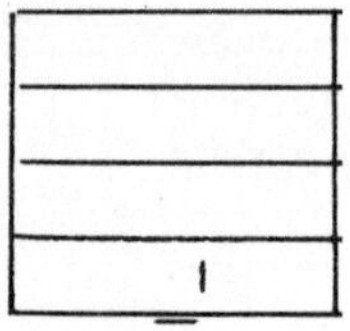

Standing on left foot with right foot in the air in front of the body at mid calf height.

Fig. 13

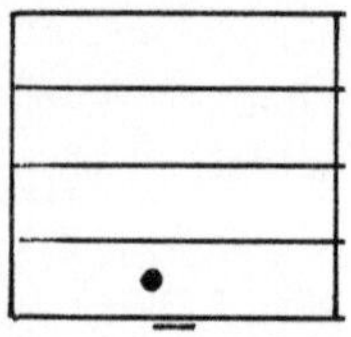

Standing on right foot with left foot in the air behind the body.

Symmetrical arm positions

Fig. 14

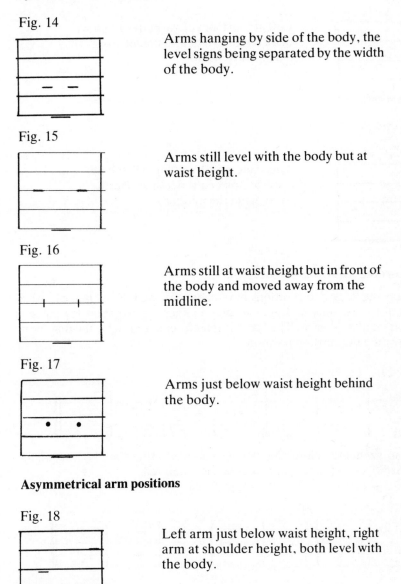

Arms hanging by side of the body, the level signs being separated by the width of the body.

Fig. 15

Arms still level with the body but at waist height.

Fig. 16

Arms still at waist height but in front of the body and moved away from the midline.

Fig. 17

Arms just below waist height behind the body.

Asymmetrical arm positions

Fig. 18

Left arm just below waist height, right arm at shoulder height, both level with the body.

Fig. 19

Left arm in front of the body just above
head height, right arm behind just
below waist height.

Fig. 20

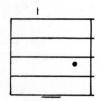

The same posture as Fig. 19, but the
arms are placed wider apart (further
away from the midline).

Recording sequences of movement

So far the recorded positions have been unrelated. From now on, when
positions are recorded next to one another the Notation is read as a
movement sequence. The stave is read from left to right, the first frame
recording the starting position.

Fig. 21

Arms swinging. Note the double bar line written at the end of the
recording to indicate that the sequence is finished.

Fig. 22

A simple leg-lifting sequence. The right leg moves in front of the body,
the left leg moves behind the body.

Redundancy avoidance

The technique of redundancy avoidance is demonstrated in the above two recordings. In Fig. 21 the feet do not move from their initial position, and are therefore not recorded in the following frames. In Fig. 22 the arms do not move and are therefore not restated. This important technique clears the stave of unnecessary information, making for speedy concise notating and clearer reading.*

Fig. 23

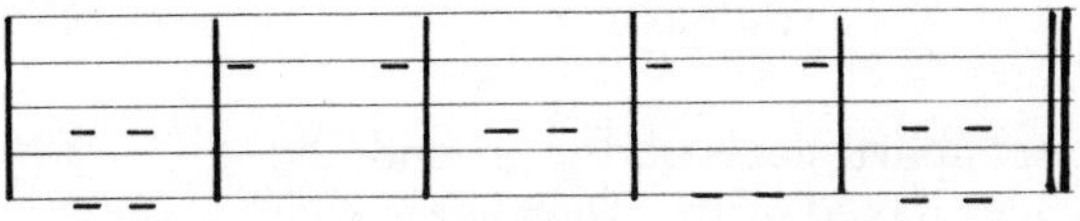

A sequence in which the arms move through the same pattern twice. During the penultimate movement the heels rise off the ground, returning to the ground during the last movement.

Notating flexed joints

The three basic signs are developed into crosses to record flexed elbows and knees. Thus:

A small vertical line is added to the level sign to form a cross, denoting a joint flexed level with the body.

A small horizontal line is added to the forward sign to form a cross, denoting a flexed joint in front of the body.

The dot becomes a cross, denoting a joint flexed behind the body.

---

* It must be noted that avoiding the duplication of information (redundancy avoidance) must be applied with great caution, otherwise the recorded information becomes unreadable and inaccurate. An example of over-use of redundancy can be seen in written shorthand which omits so much information that it is limited in its usage and development: as a shorthand it has not replaced the written language. BMN is not a shorthand.

Symmetrically flexed knee positions

Fig. 24

Feet apart, knees slightly flexed.

Fig. 25

Feet apart, heels off the ground; the knees flexed further than in Fig. 24

Fig. 26

Feet together, knees slightly flexed and touching. Note that the two flexion signs are joined.

Asymmetrical knee positions

Fig. 27

Standing on left leg, knee flexed. Right leg in the air in front of body with the knee flexed.

Fig. 28

Right foot in front and left foot behind the body, centre of gravity between the feet. Both knees flexed. Note that the right knee is in front of the body and the left knee is level with the body.

Fig. 29

Standing on the right leg, which is straight. The left leg is off the ground with the knee flexed in front of the body and the foot level with the body.

Symmetrically flexed elbow positions

Fig. 30

Elbows flexed level with the body at shoulder height, hands in front of body also at shoulder height. They are almost touching the collar bone.

Fig. 31

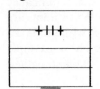

Again the hands and elbows are at shoulder height, but the elbows are in front of the body. The relationship of the hands to the elbows places the hands at a distance from the body.

Fig. 32

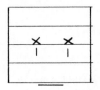

Elbows flexed above waist height behind the body. Hands at hip height in front of the body.

Asymmetrical elbow positions

Fig. 33

Left hand in front of body at shoulder height, elbow flexed at just above waist height. Right hand level with body just below waist height, and right elbow flexed behind the body above waist height. Such arm positions are found in running.

Fig. 34

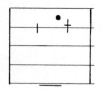

Right elbow flexed just above shoulder height in front of body with right hand at head height behind the body. Left arm is straight with hand in front of body at shoulder height, as e.g. during the movement of throwing a javelin.

Fig. 35

Redundancy avoidance, previously explained, functions in this example when recording the arms. However, it should be noted that redundancy avoidance does *not* apply when recording flexed joints. When joints are flexed they must always be recorded. An extremity sign without flexed joint information means that the limb is straight. In the above example the knees are straight in the starting position, then flex and straighten twice during the sequence.

Fig. 36

The knees are flexed in the starting position and remain flexed for the first two movements. During the last movement the knees straighten.

Fig. 37

An asymmetrical arm exercise, flexing and extending the elbows.

Extremities and joints across the body midline

Until now joints and extremities have been located in their own side of the frame. That is to say, a right arm, leg, or flexed joint has been positioned to the right of the midline, likewise a left arm, leg, or joint has been positioned to the left of the midline. But joints, and more often extremities, cross the midline in both salient positions and during movement. It is therefore necessary to have means of identifying, for example, a left extremity across the midline. The extremity or flexed joint sign which has crossed the midline is identified by a light diagonal stroke across the basic sign (note the direction of this stroke).

	level	*in front*	*behind*
Extremities crossed over the body midline.	⟋	⟋	⟍
Flexed joints crossed over the body midline.	⟋	⟋	⟍

Fig. 38

Arms in front of body at shoulder height, both hands across midline.

Fig. 39

Left elbow flexed, left hand across midline on right side of body. Right arm level with body.

Fig. 40

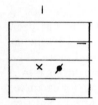

Standing on right leg, left leg in the air behind body with left knee flexed and left foot across the midline on the right side of the body (a balletic position called 'en attitude').

Fig. 41

Arms cross and uncross whilst moving higher, finishing in front of the forehead with hands crossed. Note that when the forward signs are close together one stroke is used to cross through both signs.

Fig. 42

The elbows are flexed in the starting position and remain flexed whilst the hands cross. The elbows then extend but the hands remain crossed. The last three movements are executed with straight arms.

Fig. 43

Throughout this sequence the left leg is in the air with the knee flexed. Initially only the foot crosses the midline but in the final movement both the left knee and foot move across to the right.

2. Movement Lines

A movement sequence can be considered as a series of postures, in the same way as a series of film frames which in themselves are static, produce a sequence of movement when viewed one immediately after another. Recording movement by this method would be very time-consuming to write and clumsy to read back. However, by tracing the path of an extremity (hand or foot) with a movement line as it moves from one position to another, all intermediate positions are summarized in a highly visual manner. Movement lines record the *shape* of the movement.

Movement lines recording arm movements are written within the frame.

Fig. 44

(i)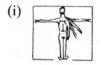
Some of the positions passed through to move the arm to shoulder height.

a)   b)

(ii)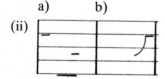
a) asymmetrical starting position
b) movement line linking starting position with finishing position

Movement level with the body (in the frontal plane)

Fig. 45

Note that movement lines are written finer than extremity signs.

Movement in front and behind the body (in the sagittal plane)

Fig. 46

The arm movements are similar to those in Fig. 21. However, they are written more efficiently with movement lines which summarize positions passed through during the swing.

Qualified movement lines

Qualified movement lines indicate whether the arms have moved in front or behind the body when passing from one position to the next.

Fig. 47

The arms move in front of the body during the first movement, and behind the body during the second. Note that the in front sign is written at right angles to the movement line for clarity.

Movement in the horizontal plane

Fig. 48

In this sequence the movement lines at * clearly indicate that the arms have crossed. It is therefore not necessary to cross out the extremity signs.

Movement lines which describe leg movements can be written in one of two ways:

1   In the stave
2   Below the stave

When written in the stave they can be recorded in the frame, or from frame to frame.

Movement lines written in the frame

Fig. 49

The right leg moves in the air, in front, to the side, and then behind the body. The left leg then moves in the opposite pattern; behind, to the side, and finally to the front of the body.

Movement lines written from frame to frame

Stepping in place (marking time)

A marking-time movement takes place on one spot. The salient positions of marking time can be notated as follows:

Fig. 50

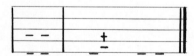

Note that the frames written along the stave have been removed, the eye now being capable of measuring them as the stave is scanned. However, the starting position is still written within a frame.

Fig. 51

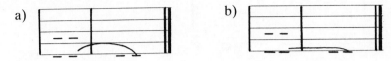

a)   b)

Fig. 51a is the same movement as recorded in Fig. 50 but notated with a movement line. The height of the movement is shown by the height of the movement line in the stave. Fig. 51b is a similar movement but it is lower than in 51a. The movement line starts over the foot that moves – in the above examples the right foot – and joins the middle of the extremity sign at the end of the movement line.

Walking

Walking is analysed here as moving from weightbearing on one foot (that is to say standing on one foot) to weightbearing on the other. To record walking forwards or backwards the | sign or ● sign is placed on the movement line.

Fig. 52

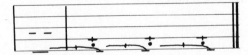

Walking forwards, commencing with the right foot. The position of the foot which is in the air at the end of each step has been recorded.

Fig. 53

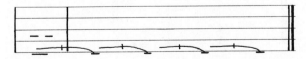

Walking forwards, commencing with the left foot. At weightbearing the foot which is behind the body need not be recorded if it is not considered relevant.

Fig. 54

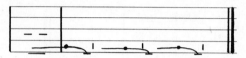

Walking backwards, commencing with the left foot.

Fig. 55

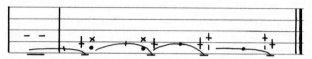

Walking both forwards and backwards with the knees flexed throughout. Note the varying step heights.

Stepping sideways

The movement line, as already stated, starts over the foot that moves. To indicate movement sideways, the end of the movement line attaches to the left end of the level sign if the movement is to the right and to the right end of the level sign if the movement is to the left.

Fig. 56

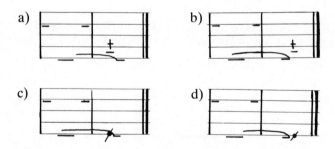

a) right foot stepping to the right.
b) left foot stepping to the left.
c) left foot stepping to the right, the right foot finishes on the left side of the midline.
d) right foot stepping to the left.

Movement lines written under the stave

Sliding

When a foot slides along the ground it is in contact with the surface throughout the movement. Sliding movement lines are written under the bottom line of the stave with straight movement lines, and do not attach to extremity signs.

Fig. 57

The right foot slides until it is in front of the body. It then slides back to its starting position, finally sliding to a position behind the body.

Fig. 58

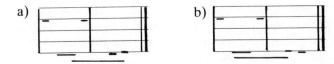

a) slide to the right keeping the weight on the left foot.
b) slide to the left keeping the weight on the right foot.

Fig. 59

Travelling forwards, sliding first the left foot then the right.

Fig. 60

Travelling backwards, sliding the feet. The right foot moves first.

Fig. 61

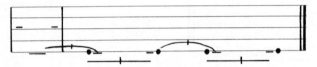

Right foot steps forwards, the left foot slides forwards, the right foot high-steps forwards, the left foot slides forwards.

Skimming

Skimming movements of the foot *just* clear the ground. The movement is so close to the ground that it is not described with a stepping movement line. Skimming movement lines follow exactly the same rules as slide lines but are written as a double line under the stave.

Fig. 62

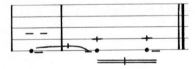

Step forwards with the left foot and skim forwards with the right foot.

Jumping

Movement lines which record jumping are written as curved movement lines below the stave.

Fig. 63

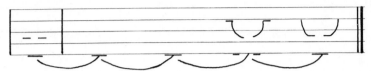

Two jumps with feet together, one jump landing with feet apart, the final jump landing with feet together. Note the arm movements during the last two jumps.

It is not necessary to record the knees flexing and extending when jumping if they function normally, as the positions are assumed.

Fig. 64

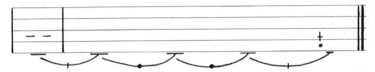

Three jumps taking off and landing on both feet, one travelling forwards, the next two travelling backwards. The fourth jump travels forwards, taking off from both feet but landing on the right foot.

Fig. 65

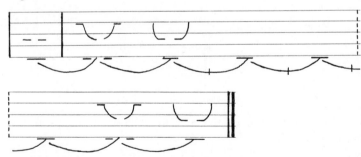

A sequence combining jumping on the spot and jumping forwards.

The previous examples have shown recordings jumping from both feet. However it is possible to stand on both feet, and just prior to moving shift the weight so that the impetus for the movement is from one foot only.

This is indicated by commencing the movement line from the left or right end of the sign.

Fig. 66

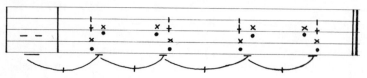

Running forwards, the impetus comes from the left foot in the starting position. Note the use of the arms in opposition with flexed elbows.

Jumping sideways is notated by attaching the movement line to the right or left end of the level sign as in previously explained sideways movements.

Fig. 67

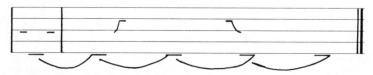

Two jumps to the right followed by two jumps to the left. All the jumps taking off and landing on both feet.

Fig. 68

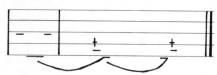

Jumping to the right landing on the right foot, then jumping to the left landing on the left foot.

Jumping with aerial positions recorded

In the previous examples the position of the legs in the air is not recorded as the flexion and extension which takes place at the knee during the take-off and landing is assumed. The legs *are* recorded if they take up a significantly different position.

Fig. 69

Fig. 70

Fig. 71

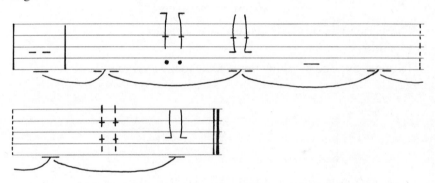

Examples of typical jumping sequences on a trampoline.

3.   *Recording the Head and Torso*

When the body midline is drawn on the stave in any of the upper three spaces it becomes possible to notate movements of the following:

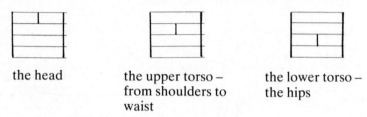

the head   the upper torso –   the lower torso –
                  from shoulders to   the hips
                  waist

There are three principal actions of the head:

1. Tilting

Tilting is notated by tilting the midline to the required side.

Fig. 72

Head tilting to the right   Head tilting to the left

2. Turning to the side (rotating)

Turning is notated by adding a horizontal line to whichever side the movement takes place.

Fig. 73

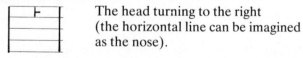   The head turning to the right
                        (the horizontal line can be imagined
                        as the nose).

3. Bending forwards and backwards (flexing and extending)

Bending is notated with a small horizontal line passing through the midline:

Fig. 74

Head bending forwards (the   Head bending backwards
horizontal line can be imagined
as the chin)

By combining these three signs all combinations of bending, tilting, and turning can be notated.

Fig. 75

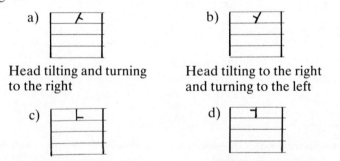

a)   Head tilting and turning   b)   Head tilting to the right
       to the right   and turning to the left

c)   Head bending forwards   d)   Head bending backwards
       and turning to the right   and turning to the left

Fig. 76

In the starting position the head is upright (therefore not notated). It bends forwards, returns to the upright position, turns to the left, returns, finally bends forwards while turning to the left. Note that the upright position *is* notated when the head *returns* to normal.

MOVEMENT OF THE TORSO

These movements are written in their respective spaces in exactly the same way as for the head:

Fig. 77

a)    b)

Upper torso tilting to the right   Upper torso turning to the right

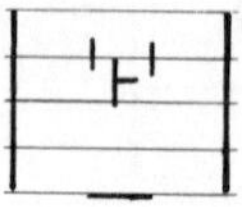

Fig. 78

a) 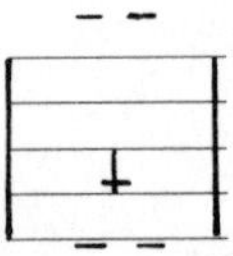   b)

Bending forwards at the hips   Hips turning to the left

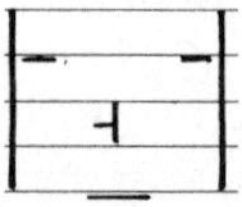

When movement occurs in the torso the body area above the movement is carried in line, e.g.

Likewise when movement occurs in the upper body or the hips the arms do not move in their own right but are carried with the torso, e.g.

COMBINED HEAD AND TORSO MOVEMENTS

Fig. 79

a)

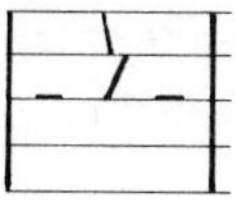

b)

c)

Upper torso tilting to
right whilst head tilts
to left

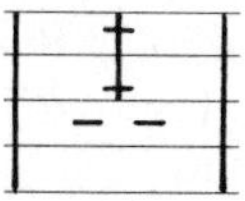

Upper torso bending
forwards whilst head
bends backwards

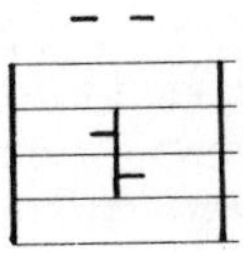

Hips turning to right
whilst upper torso
turns to left

Degrees of tilting, turning, and bending

By manipulating the signs previously described, degrees of movement are
concisely recorded.

	slight	*medium*	*full*		*slight*	*medium*	*full*
Tilting: to the right	/	/	/	to the left	\	\	\
Turning: to the right	⊢	⊢	⊢	to the left	⊣	⊣	⊣
Bending forwards	+	⊥	⊥				
Bending backwards	†	†					

Note that, since bending backwards normally has a more limited range of movement, only two degrees are recorded. Finer and more specific degrees of movement can be recorded with angle notation which is not described in this book. By combining these signs and using the varying degrees for each movement as described above, it is possible to record 792 movements of the head, upper torso, and hips.

Fig. 80

a) Full side tilt plus medium forwards bend

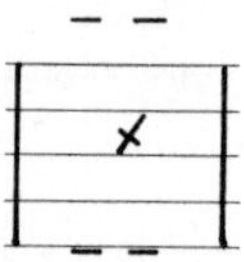

b) Medium bend forwards plus slight turning to the left

Fig. 81

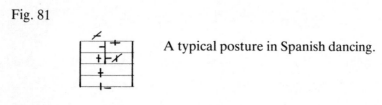

A typical posture in Spanish dancing.

Fig. 82

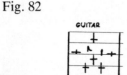

The common stance executed by pop guitarists. See Chapter 11 for recording supporting objects.

Fig. 83

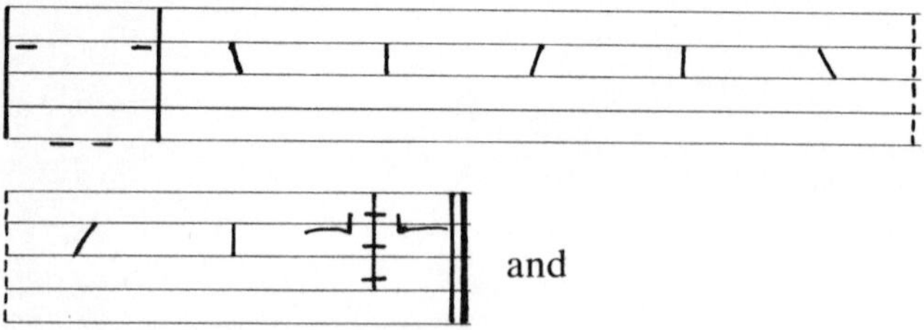

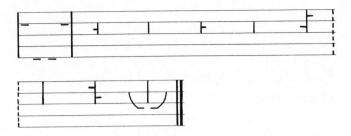

Two 'keep fit' exercises. Remember that the arms are carried with the movement of the body.

Fig. 84

An ungainly walk. The head is bent forwards throughout.

Fig. 85

A walk tipping from side to side. The head is bent forwards throughout. Additionally it tilts in compensation with the body during each step.

4. Recording Dynamics, Timing, and Direction

Dynamics

Dynamics describe the quality of movement, and in many cases the dynamic value of movement is integral to the Notation.

For example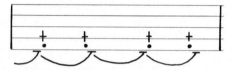

executed at great speed will automatically produce sharp staccato-like jumps.
Conversely

executed at a very slow speed will produce arm movements which are very smooth.

An essential part of dynamics or the quality of movement can be expressed by the following equation:

$$\frac{movement}{time} = dynamics$$

Therefore, in the majority of cases, the use of metronomic timing or the applicable musical term at the beginning of the stave will give the necessary information to add the dynamic value to the movement. Which of these labelling systems is used will depend on the recording language. For instance, in dance languages where a music score is associated with the recording the appropriate musical term is written at the beginning of the stave. In clinical work and in dance works executed to electronic music a metronomic beat is recorded.

However, specific postures or movements within a sequence may have differing dynamic qualities without affecting the overall timing of the recorded sequence. In such cases the expression marks which have served music so well over the centuries are adapted to record the quality of posture or movement as follows;

ppp   very very relaxed
pp   very relaxed
p   relaxed
f   strong
ff   very strong
fff   with maximum strength

Dynamics are generally written above the stave. The scope of this book limits the description of extremely detailed use of dynamics. However, the following examples show their general application.

Fig. 86   Fig. 87

A stretching position, the entire   A very floppy position
posture executed with a strong dynamic
quality

    The use of crescendo and decrescendo signs records increasing and decreasing effort of movements.

Fig. 88

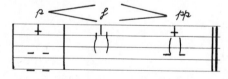

The arms and head move from a relaxed position with increasing strength. They return to the starting position with an increasingly relaxed quality.

Legato lines

One function of legato lines in the Notation is to link movements together so that the movement is continuous through all salient positions.

Fig. 89

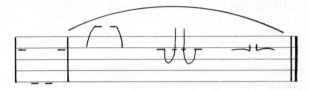

The arms move continuously from one position to the next.

Fig. 90

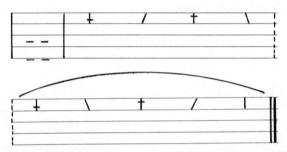

Head rolling first to the right moving specifically from position to position. When rolling the head to the left the movements are continuous.

Accents

An inaudible accent identifies a sharp movement. The sign for an inaudible accent is an inverted triangle written above the movement.

Fig. 91

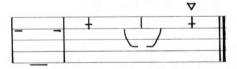

In the final movement the head bends forwards sharply, unlike the first bend.

Audible accents

When a noise is caused by a sharp movement an audible accent is recorded. The sign for an audible accent is a filled-in inverted triangle.

Fig. 92

The hands meet, as a clap. Note that the sign for hands contacting each other is derived from two forward signs slanting and touching each other (see contact signs, Chapter 6).

Fig. 93

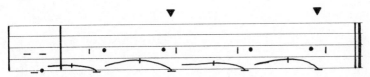

A walking sequence; a noise is made by the left foot striking the ground.

Rhythm and timing

The passage of time is common to all movement; rhythms are patterns of time. Both will be considered in this book only in general terms. Each movement of the following sequence has taken a regular beat, each taking an equal amount of time to perform.

Fig. 94

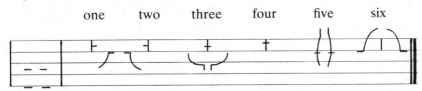

Sub beats

But it is possible that not all movements within one sequence will be of equal timing – a movement may happen halfway between one beat and the next. Such a movement occurs on a *half beat* and is identified above the stave with ▶ sign.

Fig. 95

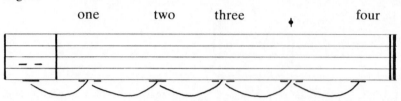

The sequence has four main beats and one half beat. The jumps that occur between three and ◆ and the ◆ and four are smaller, as they occur over less time than the other jumps.

Fig. 96

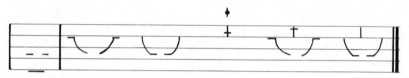

The head bends forwards on the half beat.

Further divisions of sub beats are *quarter beats* recorded with ↰ and ⸕ . *Third beats* are recorded with ↖ and ⸕ .

Fig. 97

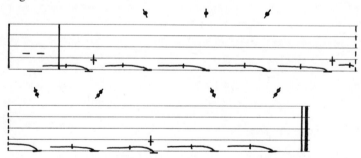

A bizarre walking sequence using quarter- and third-beat rhythms.

Pulse beats

The pulse beat ⏀ written above the stave indicates that no movement occurs at that point in the sequence.

Fig. 98

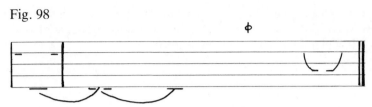

A sequence with four beats. No movement occurs on the third beat.

Fig. 99

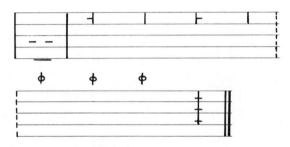

An eight-beat sequence. The long pause lasts for three beats.

Pulse beats under legato lines

When movement is executed continuously over a number of counts the required number of pulse beats is written under the legato line.

Fig. 100

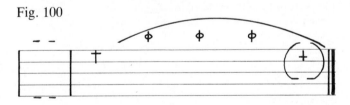

After the initial head movement the arms and head move together and continuously over four counts.

Direction

More often than not the movements of a person or a group of people relate to a direction – a worker faces his work bench, a dancer her audience. Even a morris team dancing in a village square chooses a direction which becomes 'the front'. In the Notation a direction sign indicates which way a person is facing. This sign can be thought of as an arrow ↑ in which the head is replaced by a dot ↑ .

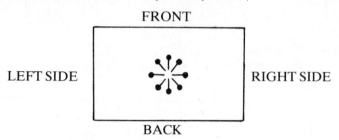

FRONT

LEFT SIDE   RIGHT SIDE

BACK

The sign is written below the stave.

| Facing the left wall | Facing the front right corner | Facing the back | Facing the front |

Note: When facing front in a starting position, there is no need to use a direction sign. However, when moving to the front from another direction, the direction sign must be used:

Turning

Turning is a change of direction – whether in the danced performance of a pirouette, a pivot in modern dance, or a child sliding in a 'bottom shuffle' on a slippery floor.

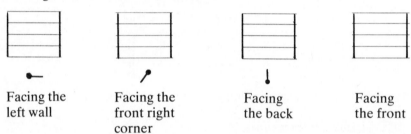

Half turns: ↑ turning clockwise to ↓ becomes ↶
              ↑ turning anticlockwise to ↓ becomes ↷

Full turns: ↑ turning a full turn clockwise becomes ↻
              ●— turning a full turn anticlockwise becomes ↺

Group formations

In dance of all kinds and in more limited usage in work study and clinical recording it is essential to have a means of recording numbers of people simultaneously. These groups are related in patterns which can be static or travelling. Patterns can be simple, such as lines or files, or they can be very complex. A variety of simple patterns will be described; the recording of this information is called 'scoring'.

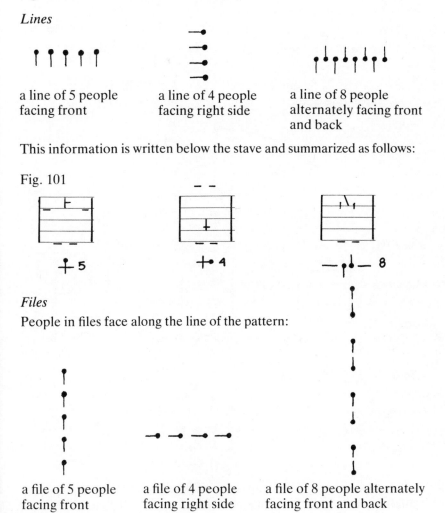

Lines

a line of 5 people
facing front

a line of 4 people
facing right side

a line of 8 people
alternately facing front
and back

This information is written below the stave and summarized as follows:

Fig. 101

Files
People in files face along the line of the pattern:

a file of 5 people
facing front

a file of 4 people
facing right side

a file of 8 people alternately
facing front and back

Fig. 102

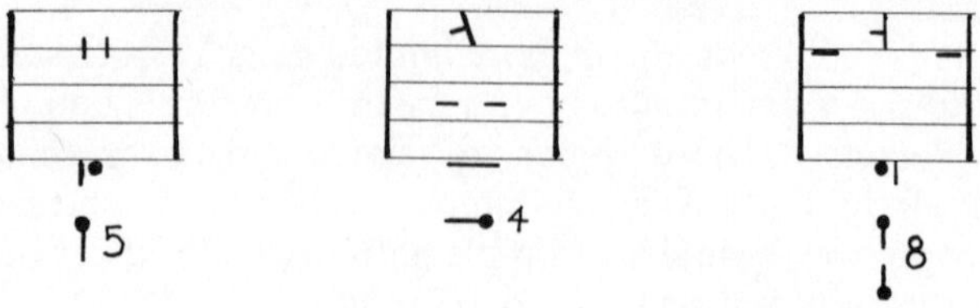

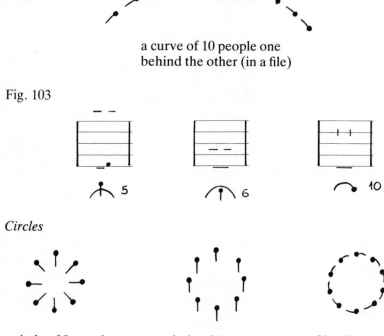

Curves

a curve of 5 people
radiating outwards

a curve of 6 people
all facing front

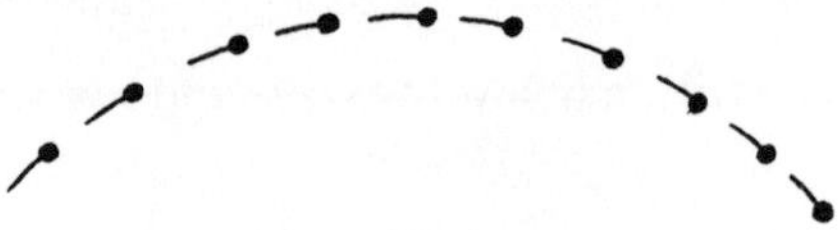

a curve of 10 people one
behind the other (in a file)

Fig. 103

Circles

a circle of 8 people
radiating outwards

a circle of 8 people
all facing front

a file of 10 people
in a circle

Fig. 104

One person travelling

When a person is travelling two elements of information must be recorded:

1   The direction the person is facing
2   The direction of travel

Both pieces of information are summarized by an arrow ↑ to which 'feathers' are added. ↕

The arrow is split into four parts, each of which gives specific information, and the direction of travel is shown by the flight of the arrow.
Travelling towards the front:

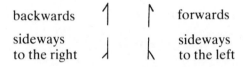

backwards   forwards

sideways   sideways
to the right   to the left

It is helpful to remember when travelling forwards and backwards, the head of the arrow is visualized as the right shoulder.
In the examples below each travelling direction sign is shown in relation to the static direction sign at the centre.

Forwards

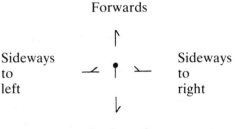

Sideways   Sideways
to   to
left   right

Backwards

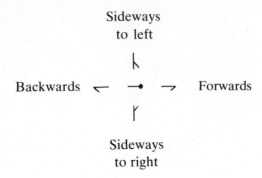

Sideways
to left

Backwards   Forwards

Sideways
to right

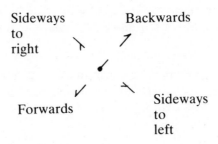

Sideways
to
right

Backwards

Forwards

Sideways
to
left

Fig. 105

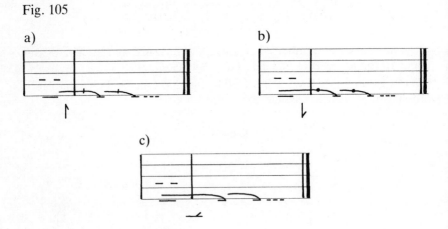

a)   b)

c)

Continuous (ad lib) walking:
a) forwards   b) backwards   c) sideways to the left

A number of people in a pattern travelling

This information is written by combining the travelling sign with the pattern. When all the people in the group are performing the same movements they can be recorded on one stave.

Fig. 106

A line of ten people facing front, travelling forwards and backwards.

Fig. 107

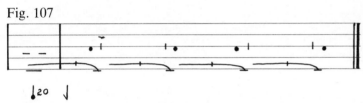

A file of twenty people marching, facing the back.

Fig. 108

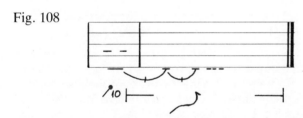

Not all travel follows a straight path. The sign can trace the path of travel. Note the brackets which encompass the time taken to complete the pattern.

Fig. 109

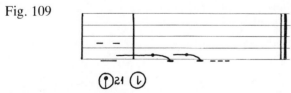

A circle of twenty-one people all facing front. The pattern of the circle is retained as they walk backwards.

Fig. 110

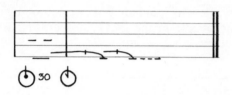

A circle of thirty people radiating inwards (all facing into the centre of the circle). As they walk forwards the circle grows smaller.

Fig. 111

Twenty people in two groups, facing each other in two lines. They move towards each other. Then group ⸉ turns by the right shoulder. At the same time group ⸋ turns by the left shoulder to form two files. They then pass each other to form files having now swapped sides. Finally they turn to face each other forming lines.

This theory develops to apply to groups of people travelling in specific areas of stages, work areas, clinics etc. The logical development of the Notation enables the most complex patterns, such as a military tattoo, to be simply and efficiently recorded.

5. Recording Lying, Sitting, and Kneeling

When lying, sitting, or kneeling, specific parts of the body are supported by the floor, chair, bed, etc. Supported signs (which are derived from the contact sign, see Chapter 6) record which body parts are supported.

Left	Right	
▬	▬	level sign
\	/	contact sign
⌐	⌐	supported sign

The derived signs tilt respectively to the left and right enabling clear identification of which side of the body is supported.

Lying

Whereas movements and postures when standing are in the vertical plane, movements and postures when lying are in the horizontal plane. Although recording in a different plane the Notation still records from behind. The horizontal plane is indicated by qualifying the direction sign with a 'floor line'. The addition of this information indicates the lying position.

Lying on one's back (supine) – the floor line is added to the back of the direction sign. ⊤

Lying on one's front (prone) – the floor line is added to the front of the direction sign. ⊤

Side lying on the left side – ⧗

Side lying on the right side – ⧗

When recording lying the following information must be notated:

1　The direction sign with the relevant 'floor line'.

2　Which body parts are supported, e.g. when lying flat the torso areas of the shoulders and hips are recorded as supported:

The head is also on the floor (if no other information is given), but there is no need to record it.

Supported signs are added to extremity signs when hands or feet are supported.

	Left extremity	*Right extremity*	
	⌐	⌐	level
	⅄	⅄	in front
	⌐•	•⌐	behind

But when the feet are recorded under the bottom line of the stave they do not require the extremity signs to carry additional supported signs, as this represents the floor area.

Lying on one's back (supine)

Fig. 112

a)

b)

Facing front, feet together on floor, arms by side on floor

Facing left, feet apart on floor, left arm at shoulder height on floor, right arm in front of body at shoulder height

Fig. 113

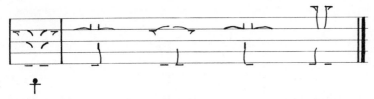

Facing front. One leg at a time lifting and returning to the floor. The arms also lift off and return to the floor. Note the new arm position in the last frame.

Fig. 114

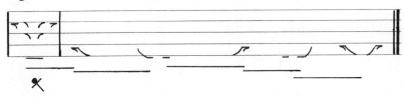

Facing front left corner. The legs slide along the floor, note the sliding movement lines.

Fig. 115

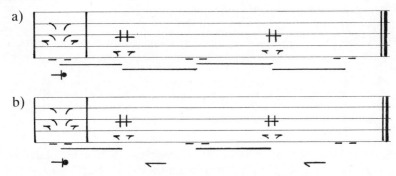

The knees flex and extend in both the above recordings. However in Fig. 115b the additional backwards travelling sign indicates that the *body* slides along the floor whilst the knees are extending.

Lying on one's front (prone)

Fig. 116

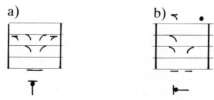

Facing front; arms at shoulder height on the floor

Facing left; right arm above head and behind body, raising the right shoulder off the floor

Fig. 117

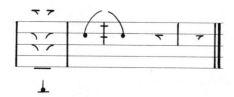

Facing back. The arms swing in an arc behind the body as the upper torso and head bend backwards (thus leaving the floor). The head, torso and arms return to the floor simultaneously.

Fig. 118

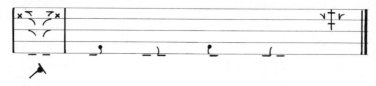

Facing front right corner. Note the elbows flexed behind the body in the starting position. In the final movement they extend as the upper body and head leave the floor.

Rolling

Fig. 119

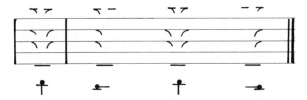

Rolling from side to side, with points of support specified.

Fig. 120

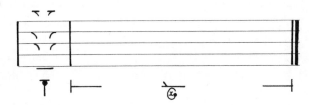

Rolling over and over is written with combined turning and travelling signs.

Sitting (on floor)

When sitting, only the hip area of the torso is supported. In a simple sitting position the feet are in front of the body.

Fig. 121

Sitting, feet in front of body. Hands by side, level and supported.

When the knees flex whilst sitting on the floor they generally rise above the waist. Consequently when recording them above the waist line of the stave, the signs could be read as representing flexed elbows.

To ensure that extremities and joints, which are recorded in that part of the stave where they would not generally be expected, cannot be confused with other extremities and joints, the 'unexpected' anatomical feature is identified with a stroke. Note that the stroke lies in the opposite direction to the stroke identifying extremities across the midline.

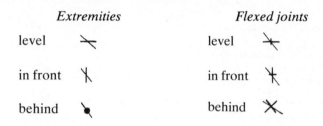

Extremities		*Flexed joints*	
level	✕	level	✕
in front	入	in front	入
behind	●	behind	✕

Fig. 122

Sitting on floor. Right leg flexes before the left. They both extend together.

Fig. 123

Sitting on floor facing left front corner. The body bends at the hips and returns to the upright twice. Finally the body moves to supine.

Sitting (on furniture)

Sitting on furniture places the feet and knees in quite different relationships to the body compared to the relationships when sitting on the floor.

In a simple sitting position on a chair the knees are approximately opposite the hips with the feet directly underneath the knees, creating a right angle at the knee joint. Both knees and feet are in front of the body. When nothing is written above the stave it is assumed that the person is sitting on the floor. However if the support is by any other means, this must be identified above the stave.

Fig. 124

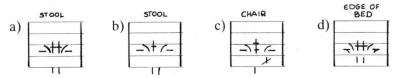

a) Sitting on stool. The knees are flexed to a right angle.
b) Similar to (a) but with the right leg completely extended.
c) Sitting on chair. Left flexed knee on top of right, causing the left leg to cross the midline (note that the flexion signs are joined one on top of the other).
d) Sitting on edge of bed. The feet are *not* touching the floor.

Fig. 125

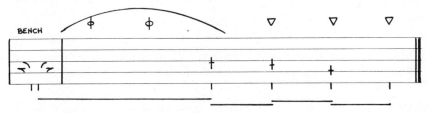

Sitting on a bench with both legs extended. The right leg flexes smoothly over three counts and then extends jerkily.

Fig. 126

Walking towards the right wall, turning to face front and finally sitting on a chair.

Upright kneeling

When kneeling upright the feet are generally behind the body.
The support signs are written hanging from the knee line.

Fig. 127

Knees apart, feet
behind body on floor

Left knee supported,
right knee flexed in
front of body at right
angles, right foot on
floor in front of body

Right knee supported,
left leg extended level
with body, foot on
floor

Fig. 128

Moving from standing to kneeling on one knee, finally moving to
kneeling on two knees.

6. Recording Contact with Self and with Another Person

The contact sign basically indicates one's own hand or foot contacting one's own body.

left   *right*

Contacting side of body

Fig. 129

a) Hands on side of thighs.
b) Left hand on shoulder, right hand on waist.
c) Standing on left leg, right foot contacting left leg at knee height.

The flexed elbows and knees are not notated as the joints must bend when hands and feet contact the body: a further example of redundancy avoidance. However, they must be recorded if their positions are considered important.

Contacting front and back of body

The basic contact sign is qualified to record contacting the front and back of the body. The 'in front' sign is added at a right angle to the contact sign to record contact with the front of the body. The 'behind' sign is developed into an open dot and added to the contact sign to record contact with the back of the body.

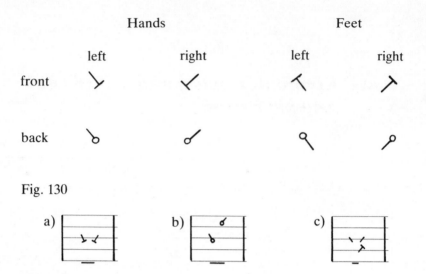

Fig. 130

a) Hands on front of waist.
b) Left hand on back of waist, right hand on back of head.
c) Hands on side of waist, standing on left leg, right foot on front of left
   knee.

It is unnecessary to cross out the contact sign when a right contacting
extremity crosses to the left or a left to the right, as the shape of the sign
gives all the information required.

Fig. 131

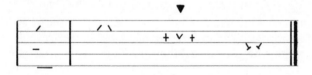

Right hand on left shoulder and left arm hanging by side, left hand to right
shoulder, clap, hands to front of hips.

One foot closing to the other

The contact sign can be added to the relevant end of the 'feet together'
sign to indicate which foot has moved into the closed position.

Fig. 132

Salute!

Fig. 133

Supine leg exercise; the moving leg closing to the non-moving leg.

Contact between two people

To record one person touching another, three different types of information need to be stated.

1.   The direction the two people are facing: When two people are standing very close together, their direction signs are written in juxtaposition and in some cases they share the same shaft. The direction signs are of different design to make for easy recognition of each person, e.g. ♀ and ♀

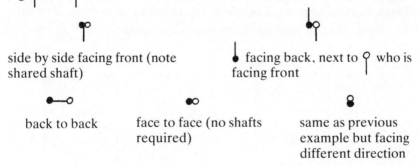

side by side facing front (note shared shaft)

♦ facing back, next to ♀ who is facing front

back to back

face to face (no shafts required)

same as previous example but facing different direction

2.   The positions and movements of the two people: The respective positions and movements of the two people are written on separate staves, each stave being identified by ♀ and ♀. The staves are written one above the other and linked by the vertical stave lines.

Fig. 134

3. The contact of one person with another: This book will only introduce hands contacting hands and hands contacting body.

The basic contact with self sign is developed to record contact with another person:

left contact with self

left contact by another

right contact with self

right contact by another

Hand-to-hand contact

The double contact sign is added to the extremity sign to show whether the contact is to the other person's right or left hand.

1. Right hand to right hand, left hand to left hand

Fig. 135

a)
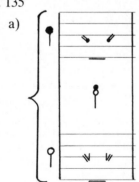

b)
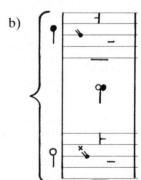

a) ↑ standing behind ↑ left hand to left hand, right hand to right hand.
b) ↑ standing on ↑'s left. Left hands in contact.
2. Right hand to left hand and left hand to right hand. Just as the contact signs record *right* hand to *left* of one's own body the double contact sign indicates a *right* hand contacting a *left* hand and vice versa.

Fig. 136

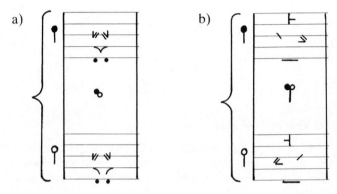

a) Kneeling facing each other, right hand to left hand, left hand to right hand.
b) Standing next to each other, holding hands.

Fig. 137   Children playing

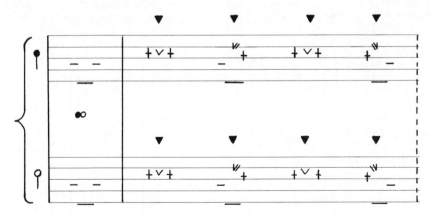

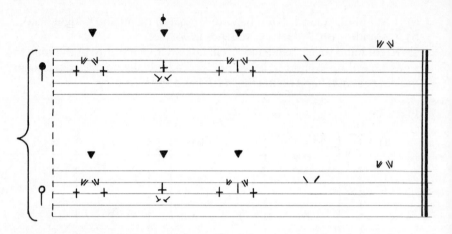

Hands contacting body of another person

When one person's hands are contacting another person's body the double contact signs are added to the basic signs as described above. Additionally, in the stave of the person whose body is being contacted, the double contact sign records where the contact is taking place. The double contact sign is qualified to show whether the contact is on the front or the back of the body in a similar way to that already described for contact with self.

                    contact level by another

                    contact in front by another

                    contact behind by another

Fig. 138

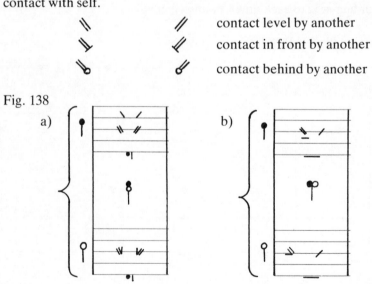

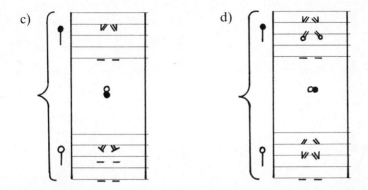

a) One behind the other, ♀'s hands contacting the side of ♂'s waist.
b) Side by side, ♀'s left hand on ♂'s waist.
c) Face to face, ♂'s hands on the front of ♀'s chest.
d) Face to face, ♂'s hands on top of ♀'s shoulders. At the same time ♀'s hands on the back of ♂'s waist.

Fig. 139

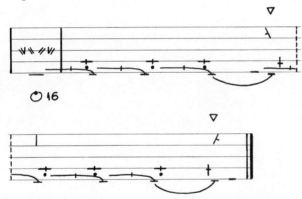

A circle of sixteen people dancing a 'Conga'.

Part Two
The Notation in Use

Preamble

The Notation described in the preceding chapters has been presented outside any specific movement language. That is to say, no understanding of a particular style of movement has been required to read the movement content in depth. In the second part of this book uses of the Notation will be described within movement languages. These are presented in alphabetical order, each movement language being described within separate chapters. However, dance has three chapters to itself due to the fact that it encompasses a number of different movement languages, and uses BMN in a variety of complex ways.

Within non-stylized movement languages, such as clinical movement or the movements found in ergonomic study, the Notation is generally used in the manner described in Part I, without further modification. When movement is used in a stylized way, the Notation is modified within the framework of the specific movement language. Where necessary, brief descriptions will be given as to how identification of the consistency of movement shapes and forms makes up the framework which leads to recognition of the languages. The parallel Notation modifications will be described.

7. *Anthropological Research*

As BMN is capable of recording any form of human movement it can be used to collect different types of movement data. However, to date the majority of anthropological movement research has been concerned with dance.

In almost all societies dance and music are integral aspects of the history and life of the community. Professor John Blacking, of Queen's University, Belfast, writes: 'there is so much music in the world that it is reasonable to suppose that music, like language and possibly religion, is a species-specific trait of man.'[1] Many would claim that like music, dance may also be common to all mankind. Dance plays an important part in many societies and a substantial amount of time can be spent in its preparation and performance. Logically, dance should be as well documented as other areas of anthropological research such as kinship, music, clothing, buildings, customs, and taboos. However, this is not the case; the anthropological study of dance is still in its infancy. Undoubtedly this is largely due to the lack of a comprehensive and, most importantly, an objective notation system. Without a suitable recording method researchers are unable to record movement data in a reliable manner which is suitable for analysis.

Verbal descriptions of movement do not convey the movement content in objective terms yet have been used on numerous occasions. A striking example appeared in the *Times* report, quoted by A. M. Franks in his publication *Social Dance.*[2] In describing the introduction of the waltz into court circles in 1816 the dance was variously recorded as 'the indecent foreign dance', 'the voluptuous intertwining of limbs' and 'this obscene display'. Similarly a researcher commenting on the dearth of information available about the Aboriginal dances of Australia noted that, although Europeans have witnessed the dances of various tribes during the last two hundred years, there is little recorded material. Most available literature

1 *How Musical Is Man?*, J. Blacking (University of Washington Press, 1973).
2 *Social Dance – a short history*, A. H. Franks (Routledge and Kegan Paul, London, 1963).

recalls the exciting atmosphere created, what the dances represented, and the splendid manner in which the dancers painted their bodies. Generally the only descriptions of the dance movements were vague references to stamps and leaps, waving of arms and shaking of knees, etc.[1] This form of description is not reliable, and objective analysis is impossible.

Dance researchers using the Notation have to solve two main problems when recording dance for anthropological study. Firstly, the movement linguistics of that particular people must be identified, the limits and vocabulary of movement varying from society to society. Secondly all the other uses, functions, and characteristics of the dance must be recognized. These aspects of anthropological study will be seen in the following descriptions of three individually and geographically separate research investigations, each demonstrating different information gleaned from study of data collected through Notation.

The dances of the Australian aborigines

The Australian aborigines, who have virtually no material culture, i.e. belongings, houses, or elaborate clothing, have, however, a rich heritage of dance, ritual, and folklore. Their stories have been written, studied, and analysed by anthropologists – but only recently has their vast store of dance been committed to paper and therefore valid study.

An Australian notator joined a research team to record the dances of various Northern Territory tribes. One aspect of establishing the specific movement linguistics became obvious when she was greatly tempted to record stamping movements simply as

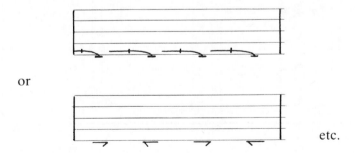

or

etc.

1 *Australian Aboriginal Heritage*, Ronald M. Berndt and E. S. Phillips, eds. (Ure Smith, Sydney, 1973).

Fig. 140

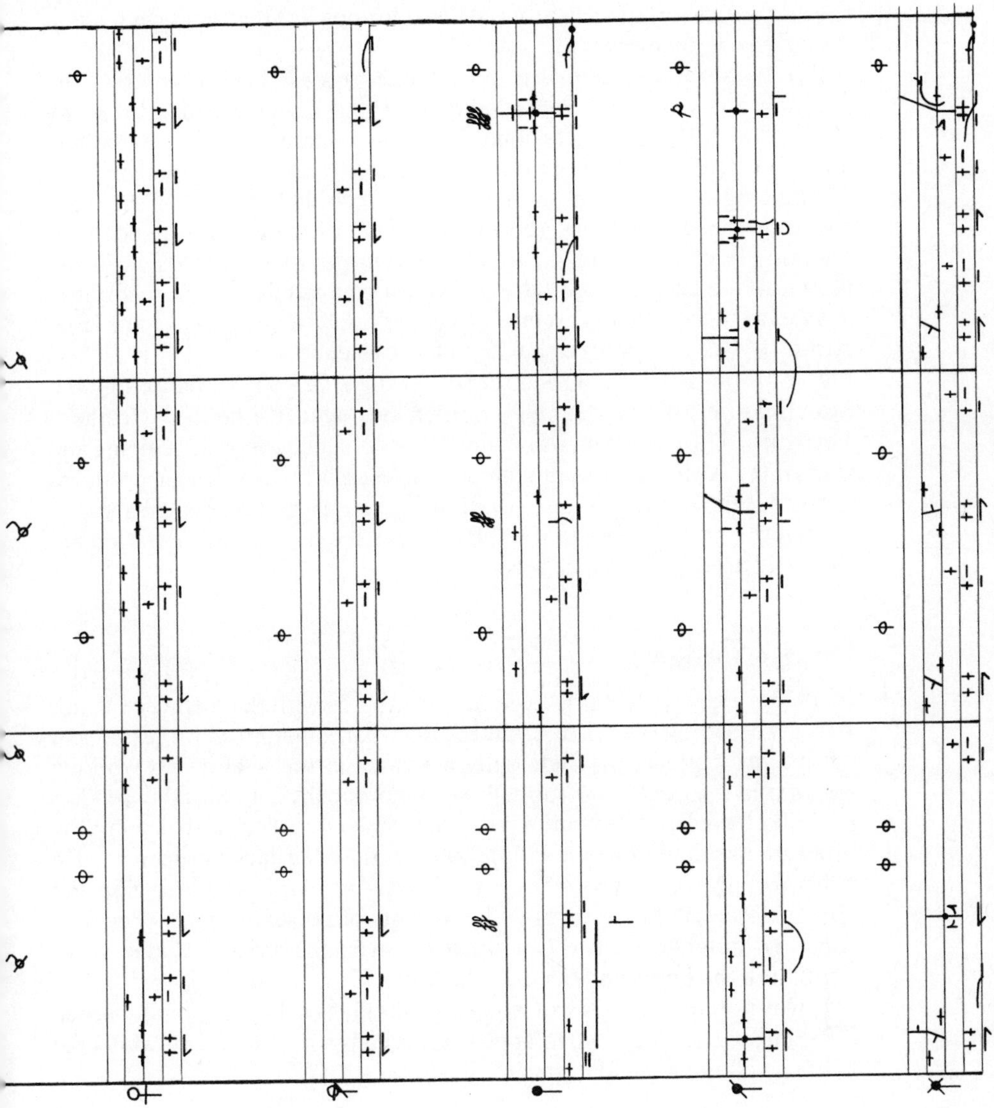

However, by making a more detailed analysis of the movement and rhythm structures of each group it became apparent that subtle individual variations were important.[1]

An essential characteristic of a dance was established through the detailed analysis of the recorded data. The researcher had spent many years previously as a professional dancer and dance notator. This initially influenced the way she notated a men's dance for a large group seemingly all dancing in much the same way. She recorded them as if she were notating the group work (corps de ballet) of a theatrical dance production. It soon became clear that this was the wrong approach, so she then notated each dancer individually. Upon analysis of these recordings it was discovered that the dance was actually led by one amongst the large group. It was conjectured that he in fact owned it.

Fig. 140, on pages 62–3, is a section of the *Black Crow*, danced by the Maiali tribe of the Bamyili Settlement near Katherine, Northern Territory. The recording shows nine dancers simultaneously jumping and stamping. Although the movements are similar, each dancer produces slight subtle variations in execution and rhythm. The first two staves record the music. Note that the bar lines used in the music notation are similarly used in the dance recording.

Dances of the Venda

In 1977 a Benesh Notator lived for six months with the Venda of South Africa recording the postures and non-verbal communication gestures of adults and children in their daily activities in the village and working sessions in the fields. Additionally she recorded the dances of the Venda.[2] It would have been difficult, if not impossible, to collect such data by any other means than movement notation. Because the data had been fixed in a form suitable for comparative analysis it was possible to link the villagers' everyday postures with concepts of personal space. (Personal space is understood in this context to mean the space included when stretching the limbs and bending the torso.)

It was noted that men and women generally use their personal space in different ways. The women appear to use a restricted amount whilst the men use all the available space.

1 Private communication from E. Allen.
2 *Some problems in the analysis of dance style with special reference to the Venda of South Africa* (1979), pp. 131–6. Andrée Grau M.A. Thesis lodged in the Department of Social Anthropology, Queen's University of Belfast.

Fig. 141   Typical standing postures

women

 hands crossed

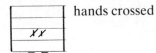 hands crossed
and held under
armpits.

men

 holding hands
with flexed
elbows.

Fig. 142   Typical sitting postures

women

 sitting on heels
with elbows on
thighs and hands
together in front
of body, leaning
forwards.

CHAIR

 sitting on chair,
elbows on knees
and hands
together leaning
forwards.

men

 sitting with
knees bent and
spread wide
apart. Elbows
on knees and
hands stretched
out in front.*

CHAIR

 sitting on chair
leaning
backwards.
Knees bent and
legs spread
wide, hands at
side.

The dances of the Venda are central to the social structure of the villagers, playing a significant part in their lives from puberty to their old age. The dances are not only specifically for different age groups but are also sex specific.

* This example demonstrates 'masking', which occurs when an extremity is directly in front of a *flexed* joint. Therefore only the flexed joint sign will be notated.

Fig. 143

A section of Tshigombela, danced by sixteen adolescent and pre-adolescent girls. Note that the flexed body posture is retained throughout and the feet do not separate widely.

Fig. 144   (see opposite)

A section of Tshikanganga, a dance for young unmarried men. Note the large body movements and the wide placing of the legs.

Through the study of the recorded data it was established that the different uses of personal space in the Venda's everyday postures were reflected in their dances.

The Sega of Mauritius

The *Sega* is promoted as the folk music and dance of Mauritius. The island had been an isolated 'sugar colony' until World War II when, with the establishment of air and naval bases, it suddenly came into contact

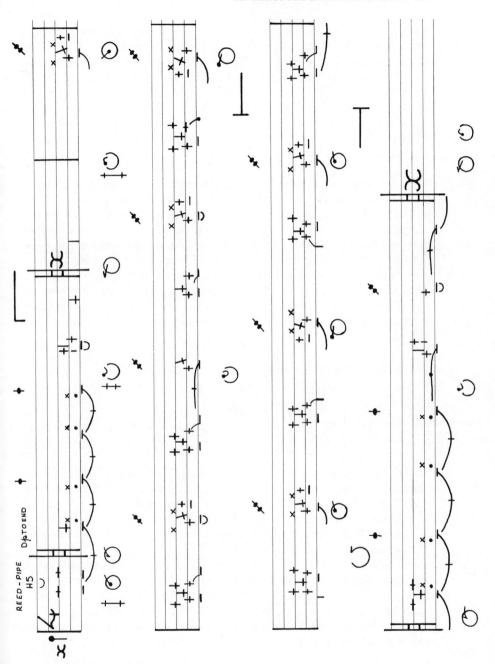

with the wider world. Tourism became an important factor in the life and economy of the island following the building of a commercial airport. The socio-economic changes and the new demands that tourism imposed inevitably led to changes in the form and function of the Sega. In 1980 an anthropological researcher set out to trace the history of Sega and through the analysis of notated recordings of the dance, to discern how the dance form had altered to meet the needs of the changing society.[1]

The peopling of Mauritius has occurred in waves of immigration throughout her history. Many Africans were brought as slaves to work in the sugar fields and today it is their descendants who form the second-largest community on the island. It is from them that the Sega emerged and until recently it was only they who performed it. At the present time the dance has several different faces but the two extreme types are the Typique, the traditional form, and Sexy, the innovated showbiz version which serves to entertain the tourists and foreign dignitaries. Sega Typique provides self-entertainment for a small group of friends or a village. The dance is accompanied by traditional percussion instruments and is a partner dance which is improvised and has no set formations or sequence. Usually danced out of doors around a fire, which is used to heat and keep taut the skins of the drums, the dancers' focus of attention is on the partner.

Fig. 145   (Simplified notation)

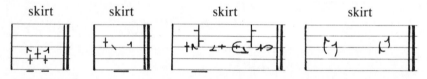

Characteristic positions and movements of the female Sega Typique dancer. The signs added to the extremity signs record supporting. (See Chapter 11 for recording supporting.) The feet are flat on the ground, the knees bent and the body flexed, each contributing to the 'enclosed' feeling of the stance. Compare these postures to the analysed postures of the Venda (page 66).

Although many characteristics of African dance are retained, such as the relaxed knees, slightly flexed torso and movements which keep close to the ground, it is interesting to note the total lack of hierarchical organization (such as in the dances of the Venda). There are no age or sex specific dances, and no leaders or followers. This would seem to reflect the loss of tribal and social organization during slavery.

1   *The Sega of Mauritius* (1980), pp. 150, 154, 156, Julie Jones M.A. Thesis lodged in the Department of Social Anthropology, Queen's University of Belfast.

Fig. 146

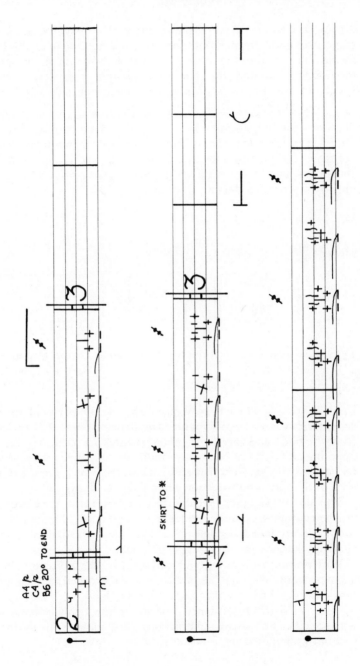

An extract from a Sega Typique dance (Fig. 146). Note the enclosed stance retained throughout: the arms are held near to the body with flexed elbows, the knees are bent with feet flat on the ground. Torso movement is limited; the sign in the hip area of the stave (between the waist and knee lines), records hip movement from side to side.

Sega Sexy came into being during the 1960s as an answer to the tourists' demands for the 'ethnic touch'. It is performed by paid dancers at the hotels in front of an audience. It is a cabaret-type presentation with great emphasis on creating interesting formations and group patterns, and is choreographed in the main for groups of pretty girls. No longer is it an improvised partner dance.

Fig. 147

skirt   skirt   skirt

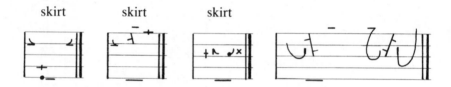

Typical postures and movements of the female Sega Sexy dancer.

Fig. 148   (see opposite and p. 72)

Extract from a Sega Sexy dance. The use of personal space differs considerably from Sega Typique. The stance is open, the arms held away from the body and various kneeling postures are used. At * the dancer is kneeling and bending backwards until her head touches the ground. Hip movement thrusts forwards and backwards. This is recorded in the hip area of the stave (between the waist and knee lines).

The above examples reveal how Sega movements have been modified and sensationalized to be interesting to audiences. Through the study of the recorded data it becomes clear that due to the dancers' stance being changed the movements have become subtly altered.

With notation it is now possible to record and easily assess all aspects of a dance event. Through the careful study of recorded data significant facts may emerge. Analysis may reveal aspects which at first may appear as an undisciplined frenzy of dance, but are in fact highly ordered structures with specific aims, uses, and functions. Most importantly the inextricable link between dance and its society can be shown.

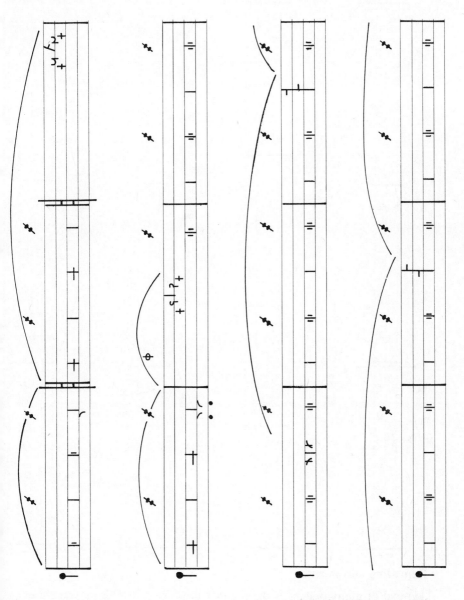

(continued on page 72)

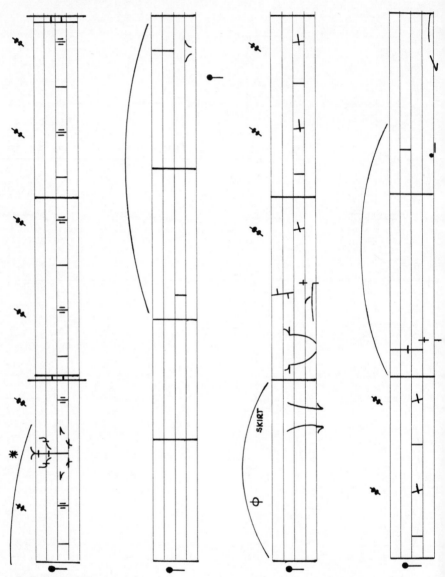

Repeating movements

Typical of many dances is the manner in which a specific movement or movement sequence is repeated over and over again. The technique of repeat signs in the Notation makes the recording of these repetitious sequences simple and extremely efficient. Repeat signs enclose information and give one of three instructions:

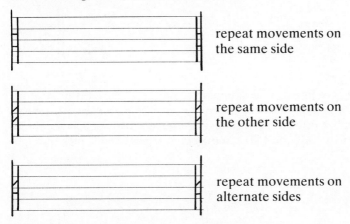

repeat movements on
the same side

repeat movements on
the other side

repeat movements on
alternate sides

Note the additional length of the outside brackets and the design of the small lines drawn inside the parallel lines.

Fig. 149

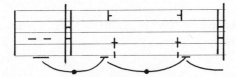

The repeat signs instruct: repeat on the same side. Therefore the repeat will be exactly the same series of movements.

Fig. 150

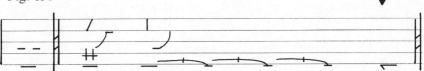

The repeat signs instruct: repeat on the other side. Therefore the repeat will be:

Fig. 151

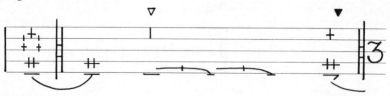

This jumping, stepping, and stamping sequence is enclosed in a set of repeat signs which instruct 'repeat on the same side'. Outside the repeat signs the number three indicates that the sequence is to be repeated three times. That is to say, the entire sequence is danced four times through altogether.

Fig. 152

The repeat signs instruct 'repeat on alternate sides', the entire sequence is danced eight times.

Fig. 153

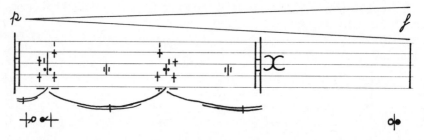

Section of a traditional dance from the Lango district of Uganda. The number of repeats is indefinite. The information under the stave indicates that the two lines of dancers +∘ and •+ start as two distinct groups and finish very close together forming one group. This distance will condition the number of repeats. Note the crescendo marking above the stave, indicating that the movements increase in tension as the dance progresses.

8. Clinical Usage

Benesh Movement Notation is a recording tool neutral to all theories of movement; thus posture and movement data captured in Notation are in a form suitable for submission to analysis and measurement for clinical recording and research purposes.

In areas such as physiotherapy, occupational therapy, paediatrics, neurology, and orthopaedics much of the posture and movement information required is gained through visual observation. It is therefore essential that clinicians should be able to observe, analyse, and record accurately and speedily the various and complex patterns for future reference. Obviously such skills must be developed to the highest degree possible. BMN, based upon the principles of visual perception and kinaesthetic image, offers a logical and scientific method of training the eye to a highly disciplined level. Heightened powers of observation are inherent in the learning process of the Notation – even at the most elementary stage. The Institute of Choreology has prepared syllabuses at varying levels which are appropriate for both students of Kinesiology and for the more experienced clinicians who wish to describe movement. Presenting movement in a concise and visual form means that function can be studied in detail, and normal and abnormal movement patterns can be assessed.

Recordings from a Kinesiology syllabus

Fig. 154

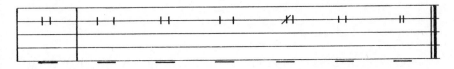

A sequence recording fine changing relationships of the arms to the body.

Fig. 155

a)

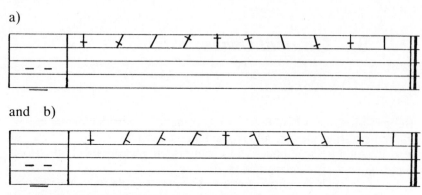

and   b)

Two examples of head rolling. Fig. 155a The head moves through combinations of flexion/extension and side tilt. In Fig. 155b rotation also occurs.

Fig. 156

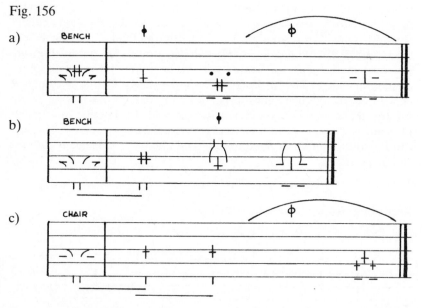

a) BENCH

b) BENCH

c) CHAIR

Three ways of rising from sitting to standing. In Fig. 156a and (b) the arms function during the movement. The knees extend at full weight bearing. However, in Fig. 156c the arms are not used and the knees do not extend.

Fig. 157

a)
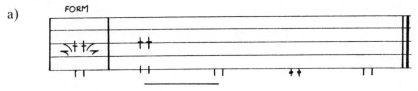

b)
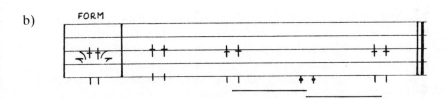

Two ankle exercises. In both sequences the penultimate movements are dorsiflexion. (See Chapter 11 for recording dorsiflexion.)

BMN in note-taking and for training

Busy clinicians occasionally take leave of absence from their units to attend specialized post-graduate courses. For example, physiotherapists attend courses in manipulation and mobilization, treatment of adult hemiplegia, handling techniques for handicapped children, and Proprioceptive Neuromuscular Facilitation (PNF). These intensive courses require detailed study of the theory presented. Note-taking is generally essential and here the problems of limited information recorded with pin men, sketches, and long-hand notes often arise. With BMN it is possible to make precise recordings of movement sequences, interactions, and techniques during lecture demonstrations.

The authors of *PNF Patterns and Techniques* state in their preface: 'Unfortunately, imparting a skill through the written word is difficult.'[1] It is possible to cut down the written word dramatically if the movement patterns are recorded in BMN.

1 *Proprioceptive Neuromuscular Facilitation Patterns and Techniques*, Knott M. and Voss D. E. (Harper and Row, 1968).

Fig. 158   PNF – Lower extremity pattern

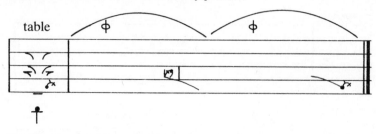

Facilitation of this pattern is achieved with the patient lying supine on a table. The leg is extended over the edge, abducted and internally rotated. The foot is in a plantar flexed and everted position. By the end of the first movement the leg has crossed the midline and externally rotated. The foot is dorsiflexed and inverted.* The second movement returns the leg and foot to the starting position. The movements are smoothly executed.

Fig. 159   PNF – upper extremity action

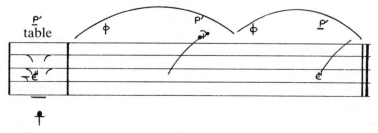

Again the patient is lying supine on a table. The arm is across the midline with the wrist flexed. The hand is clenched with ulna deviation. By the end of the first movement the arm is elevated and abducted to a position behind the body. The fingers and wrist are extended with radial deviation functioning.** The second movement returns the arm and hand to the starting position. The movements are executed smoothly.

The above examples demonstrate the efficiency of the Notation. One stave describes complex movement patterns in detail and in measurable form, whereas the accompanying verbal descriptions are lengthy and cumbersome. Similarly two-stave recording is equally efficient in recording simultaneous patient and clinician movement.

* Detailed Notation describing ankle and wrist function is outside the scope of this book. Such recording will be described in a later publication.
** The recording of finger function is described at the end of this chapter.

Fig. 160

Bobath approach – facilitation of the neck righting reflexes, supine to standing. The top stave records the patient and the bottom stave the physiotherapist.

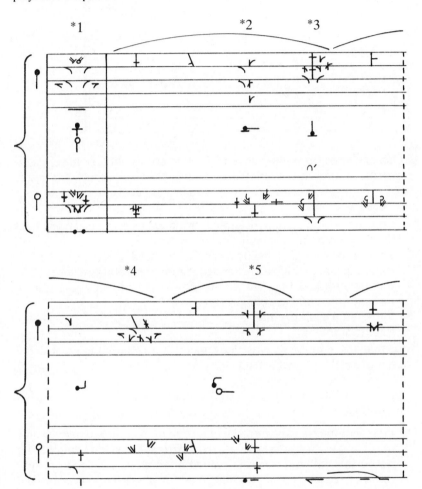

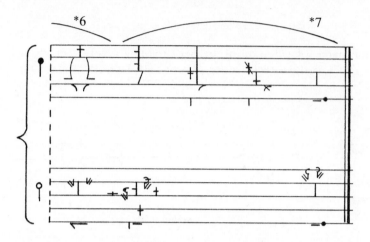

This extremely complex movement sequence would take many pages of words to describe even partially: the Notation speaks for itself. However to assist with reading, salient moments are noted with numbered asterisks:

*1. Starting positions: patient supine, front and back of head being held by therapist, who is kneeling behind patient.
*2. Patient rolls to side lying by facilitation of head.
*3. Patient prone, with back extended, hands and elbows on floor.
*4. Patient 'crook' sitting.
*5. Patient four-point kneeling.
*6. Patient upright kneeling.
*7. Patient standing.

Note that the therapist's wrist movements are recorded in great detail when moving the patient's head.

Gait analysis

The dearth of measurable movement information in clinical notes is only too well known. In a survey of elderly bilateral lower limb amputees it was noted that full and accurate patient information on blood pressure etc. could be retrieved from hospital notes, but physiotherapy records did not provide enough movement detail.[1]

This lack of information exists because no one accepted recording

1 'A pilot survey of elderly bilateral lower limb amputees', C. Van de Ven, *Physiotherapy* (October 1973).

technique is in universal use. With BMN this problem can be overcome with BMN stave assessment sheets incorporated into the patient's file. Records of any posture or movement patterns may be recorded, e.g. sitting postures, crawling patterns, arm function, and gait. Examples of gait will be described and analysed. Fig. 160a and (b) are abstracted from the clinical recordings of the same patient, the complex gaits being notated some seven months apart. Although the following topics have not been described in this volume they have been included in the recordings: gait speed, stride width, step length, and complex hip function.

Fig. 161

a)

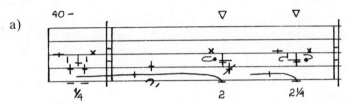

b)

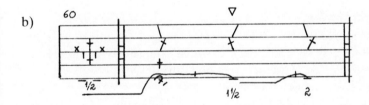

Starting posture

	Fig. 161 a	Fig. 161 b
Torso	Hip flexion	Hip flexion plus upper torso extension
Arms	Asymmetrically flexed posture	Symmetrically flexed posture
Stride width	Minimal	Increased
Knees	Flexed	No flexion

Left swing phase

Clears the ground. Half-way through the phase the right foot plantar flexes and leg externally rotates.

At beginning of phase foot drags through, clearing the ground approx. one third of the way through phase. Half way through phase right foot plantar flexes, and everts, leg externally rotates. At the same time upper torso side tilts to the right retaining the extension and the head side tilts to the left.

Left weight bearing

Left knee flexes and internal rotation functions. The pelvis displaces to the right whilst retaining the hip flexion.

Knee functions normally. Upper torso side tilts to the left whilst extension is retained. Head side tilts to the right.

Right swing phase

Normal pattern.

Drags through before clearing the ground.

Right weight bearing

Pelvis displaces to the left whilst retaining the hip flexion.

Upper torso side tilts to the right whilst extension is retained. Head side tilts to the left.

Arm function

Bizarre arm pattern swinging in the horizontal plane.

No arm function.

Step length

Asymmetrical, right longer than the left.

Asymmetrical, but less than in the a) recording, right longer than the left.

Gait speed

Approx. 40 swing phases per minute.

Approx. 60 swing phases per minute.

Recording movement data for research purposes

The Notation enables movement data to be collected across a group of subjects, thus permitting the results to be studied and compared. In this way a vertical study can be carried out in which one person's overall performance in a series of activities is assessed. And a horizontal study of recordings of the same activity performed by a number of persons can also be made.

One such study recently undertaken concerned the assessment of fundamental abilities in a group of severely mentally handicapped children. They were recorded over a period of three months performing a series of simple activities.[1] It was anticipated that each of twenty selected activities could be used to give an indication of the level of motor development of the children. As well as the three basic ability activities shown below, lying to standing, stepping on and off stairs, sitting down, rising to standing, and reaching and bending to pick things up were also recorded.

Selected recordings of children's performances in three of the fundamental ability tests are shown with accompanying notes of the sort of information that could be extracted from the recordings in order to make a developmental assessment. The following examples from the recorded data are simplified for the purposes of this book. Additionally notation of speed of function, complex dynamics, complex ankle, wrist and finger function, as well as eye and mouth movements, are not included.

Fig. 162   Jumping off both feet

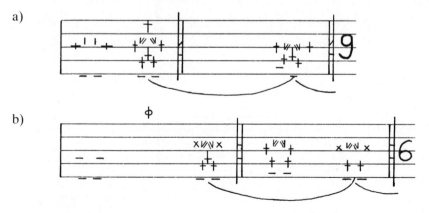

a)

b)

1   *Fundamental Movement Activities* (1977). V. J. Ashford, IOC Library.

c)

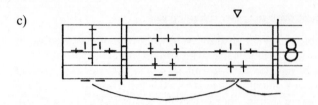

Subject A jumped from one foot to the other but required assistance to perform the test.

Subject B jumped off both feet but required assistance.

Subject C performed 9 jumps off both feet without assistance but landed heavily.

Fig. 163   Throwing a ball

a)

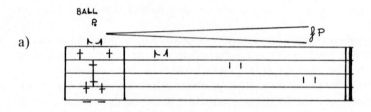

b)

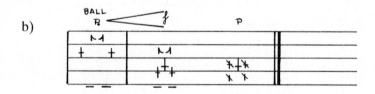

c)   i)

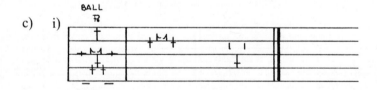

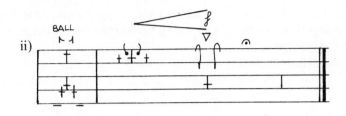

ii)

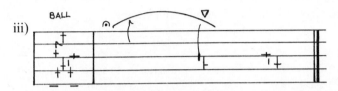

iii)

Subject A stood with body square and fingers spread around the ball. No use was made of body movements, the thrust came purely from the forearms and shoulders. Maximum strength was reached well after the release of the ball.

Subject B stood with body square. A strong hurling action was used which reached maximum strength as the ball was released. This was accompanied by flexing at the hips and knees.

Subject C this subject produced a variety of throws. The first was a double-handed throw reinforced by hip flexion. The second, a strong double-handed overarm action, again making use of the trunk. The last was a single left-handed overarm action with follow through accompanied by trunk rotation but no foot action.

Finger function

E. G. Cantrell, Senior Lecturer in Rehabilitation, notes that immuno-logical and blood tests indicate something about the progress of the rheumatoid disease of the hand but are little use as a guide to the function of the affected extremity. He goes on to point out that for an accurate clinical description, an interested therapist would need to record several pages of information, using a considerable amount of time and paper, to produce a description of hand function which would be of any use for assessment at a later date (possibly many months hence).[1]

1 'Natural history of the Rheumatoid Hand', E. G. Cantrell, *Physiotherapy* (September 1977).

Detailed hand function can be concisely described with BMN. The Notation is logically developed to permit gross and fine finger posture and movement to be recorded.

Gross finger posture and movement. The letter P denotes the fingers and thumb, and sometimes the whole hand. This letter is written above the stave.

P plus the 'in front' sign. When the fingers and thumb bend forwards, that is to say towards the palm of the hand from the neutral, the | sign is placed at a specific point on the P to denote the degree of flexion. The sign is turned sideways so it can be manipulated on the P.

P   P̄   P̄   P̄   P̱   P̱

neutral   minimally   ¼ flexed   ½ flexed   ¾ flexed   fully flexed
          flexed

If the letter P refers to the right hand, it is qualified with a tick placed to the right of the letter P´. If qualified with a tick to the left, `P a left hand is identified. However, if the letter is referring to both hands no ticks are required.

Fig. 164

Arms in front of body at shoulder height. Both hands fully clenched.

Fig. 165

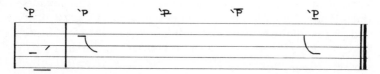

Starting position; right hand on hip, left hand by side fully clenched. As left arm moves fingers extend to normal. In the level position at shoulder height the fingers half flex, minimally flex, and fully flex as the arm returns to the starting position.

P plus the 'behind' sign. The ● denotes three different actions of the fingers and thumb.
1. Extension beyond the neutral. The sign is written through the P.

Fig. 166

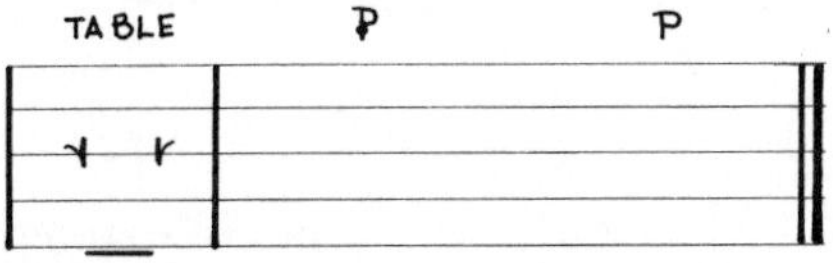

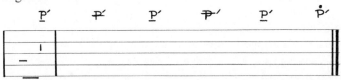

Hands supported on table. Fingers and thumbs extend and return to neutral. They in fact lift off and return to the table. The palm of hands do *not* lift off the table.

2. Rigidly held in the neutral position. The sign is written at the top of the P.

Fig. 167

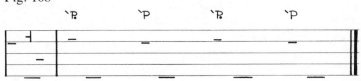

Right hand commences fully clenched. It moves through a pattern with an increasing range of flexion and extension, returning twice to the fully clenched position, finally extending to the rigid position.
3. Abduction of the fingers and thumb (spreading). The dot is written to the side of the P.

Fig. 168

Fingers and thumb of left hand spreading and closing (abduction and adduction) as the arm moves slightly.

The two signs can be used in combination to record more complex positions of the fingers and thumb:

Fingers ½ flexed and
spread

Fingers rigidly held in
the neutral position
and spread

Fingers extended
beyond the neutral
and spread

Fingers extended
beyond the neutral, ¼
flexed and spread

Fine finger and thumb posture and movement

Each digit can be recorded individually, and is identified by the following
numbers:

6 the thumb
2 the index finger
3 the middle finger
4 the ring finger
5 the little finger

The theory described above is applied in exactly the same way to each
number.

Individual digits plus the | sign

Fig. 169

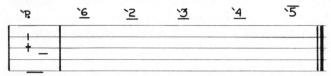

From a starting position with all fingers and the thumb spread, one finger
at a time flexes. Note that the little finger flexes only minimally.

Individual digits plus the ● sign

Fig. 170

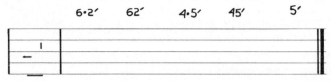

The thumb abducts (spreads), then returns to position next to index finger, the same movement occurs between the ring and little finger. Finally the little finger extends beyond the neutral.

Fig. 171

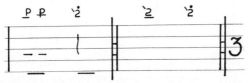

In the starting position the hands are asymmetrically flexed. As the left arm moves forwards, the index finger points stiffly, then flexes.

By further manipulation the signs develop to record the manner in which the fingers of one hand touch the fingers of the other, the way individual fingers function in grasping and the degree of flexion in each joint.

In the study of non-verbal communication and sign languages BMN has proved to be invaluable in recording the fine detail of hand shape and function. The following examples from a non-verbal communication system, British Sign Language,[1] demonstrate how efficiently the Notation signs record complex hand and finger patterns.

Fig. 172

'to know' – fingers clenched, thumb abducted and rigid, touching the front of the forehead.

Fig. 173

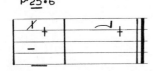

'clever' – hand position the same as Fig. 172. Hand moves across the front of the forehead.

1   The British Sign Language as used with the Makaton Vocabulary.

Fig. 174

'to understand' – flicking movement of thumb and index finger at side of temple.

Fig. 175

'dinner' – second and third finger of each hand are held rigid whilst the others are clenched.

Fig. 176

'good' – thumb is rigid and abducted whilst the fingers are clenched.

Fig. 177

'bad'. Fingers and thumb clenched but the little finger is rigid.

Fig. 178

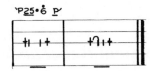

'more' (of anything) – left hand moves towards the right in a curved pattern.

Fig. 179

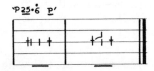

'more food' – left hand moves towards the right, finishing in a position above it.

Comparison of some recording techniques used in the clinical situation

Verbal descriptions of movement, used ubiquitously in the clinic, are incomplete and cumbersome. Furthermore, such notes are 'personal shorthands' and generally are not clearly understood by anyone other than the author. Film and video recordings are only a means of storing visual phenomena.[1] They do not permit measurement or analysis of posture and movement data except by techniques such as painstaking computer processing. Further, to observe and memorize particular aspects of recordings, repeated playing of the tapes is generally required. Access to data recorded in BMN is simple and speedy irrespective of the complexity of the movement content since it is presented in analysed (dissected) form. With notated data direct comparative analysis between different recordings is easily achieved, whereas such comparisons can only be carried out with video recordings through complex techniques such as split screen recordings. There is no distortion in notated data. This phenomenon, which creates false information, is common in video recording.

1   'A graphic method of recording normal and abnormal movement patterns', Comparetti A. M. and Gidoni E. A., *Developmental Medicine and Child Neurology*, Vol 10, No. 5 (1968).

9. Recording Classical Ballet and Contemporary Dance

When dance forms are recorded the notator and the reader of the Notation must be acquainted and familiar with the particular dance language. Certain specifics of the language are understood and are not notated in the body of the recording, making both the writing and reading of the dance score extremely efficient. In this and the following chapters examples of this technique are described where appropriate.

Classical ballet

The 'language' of Western classical ballet is understood by students and dancers no matter where they received their dance training. Such aspects as the 'turn-out' of the legs, the curved soft manner in which the arms, wrists, and fingers are held and the direction the wrists face in different arm positions are understood. Additionally, sequences of movement are linked together in specific ways and are codified by definitive names. When recording in the classical ballet language the Notation utilizes these conventions, thus presenting the movement content with great clarity, and clearing the score of unnecessary information.

Fig. 180

a) A classical retiré. The knee position and the direction of the wrists are understood within the language and therefore are not recorded.
b) A retiré. Both the flexed knee and direction of the wrists are recorded as they are in positions which are not part of the conventional classical language.

The positions of the feet are codified within the technique and are performed with the feet 'turned-out'. This 'turn-out' is understood and is therefore not recorded, e.g.

Fig. 181

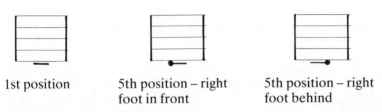

| 1st position | 5th position – right foot in front | 5th position – right foot behind |

These combined signs recording fifth position of the feet are developed to record one foot closing into the position. The 'in front sign' identifies a foot closing in front. The dot, developed into an open dot, identifies a foot closing behind.

Fig. 182

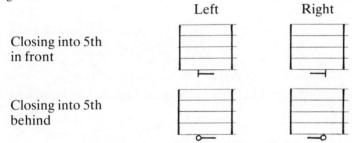

Left   Right

Closing into 5th in front

Closing into 5th behind

As mentioned previously (in Chapter 7), when recording dance the stave is divided into bars as in a music score. Additionally the number of beats in a bar is stated at the beginning of the stave. The following three figures are sequences which would be danced in the classroom.

Fig. 183

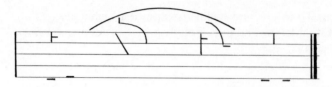

Plié in first with port de bras, pointe tendue à la seconde – the first section of a plié exercise. The left hand is supported by the barre.

Fig. 184

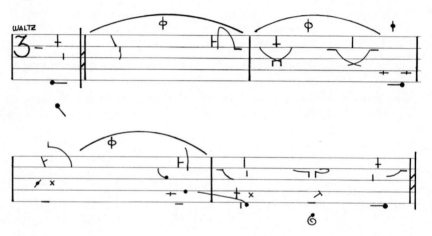

A simple port de bras and pirouette exercise repeated on the other side

Fig. 185

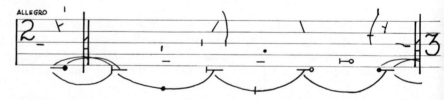

A section from a Grande Allegro sequence. Pas de chat, two sissonnes, and changement battu.

It has already been mentioned that the classical ballet language has codified movements which are linked together. If the Notation were always to record these linked steps in analysed form, it would be inefficient to write and slow to read back. Therefore, where intermediate timing is not a significant factor short forms of these codified steps are recorded.

Fig. 186

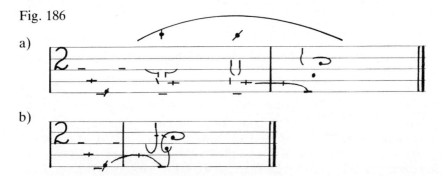

a) Posé into arabesque with timing and salient positions recorded in detail.
b) The short form – the salient intermediate positions are incorporated in the movement lines.

Fig. 187

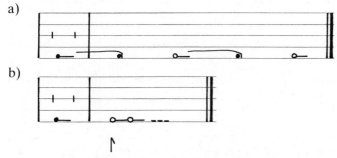

a) An analysed form of bourrée forwards.
b) The short form using the travelling sign to indicate the direction of travel.

Fig. 188

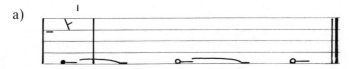

b)

a) An analysed form of bourrée sideways.
b) The short form. Once again the travelling sign indicates the direction of travel.

Contemporary dance

Within contemporary or modern dance there is a very wide variety of styles often associated with an individual choreographer. Each style can be considered a movement language. To assist in the identification of the choreographic style certain aspects of detail may be recorded at the beginning of the dance score.

Contractions of the spine are central to a majority of these dance styles. They are body movements involving the backward curving of the spine. That is to say the body rounds in a shape *behind* the neutral upright position. A contraction is recorded by adding a dot to the midline.

Fig. 189

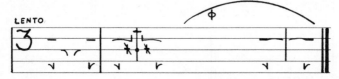

Sitting on the floor, legs apart and arms at shoulder height. As the contraction is performed the head and arms change position and the knees flex. The contraction is released and the arms and legs return to their starting positions over counts two and three.

Fig. 190

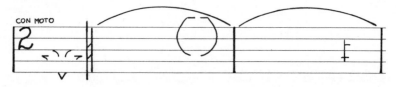

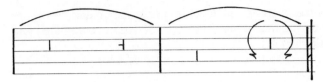

Sitting on floor, feet together. In bars one and two the pulse beats under the legato lines are redundant as the number of beats in the bar is stated at the beginning of the stave. In the final bar not only are the body movements smoothly executed but the arms move through two counts.

Fig. 191

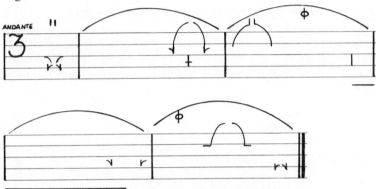

Sitting on floor, crossed-legged. The knee positions are anatomically conditioned, there is no need to record them. In the penultimate bar the knees straighten as the feet uncross and slide. In the final bar they slide back to their starting positions.

Fig. 192

A jumping sequence commencing facing front right corner. On the third count of bar one the jump turns to the right finishing facing the front left corner. The final jump travels forwards.

Low runs with the head on one level (not bobbing up and down) are used in many modern dance styles. They are notated by combining jump lines with skimming lines.

Fig. 193

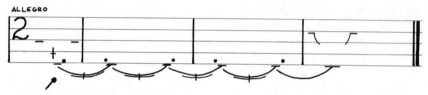

Facing front right corner. Four skim runs to corner, one jump on the spot finishing on both feet.

When writing a score, it is often convenient to write the analysed form of a much used sequence at the beginning of the score and use the short form in the body of the work.

Fig. 194

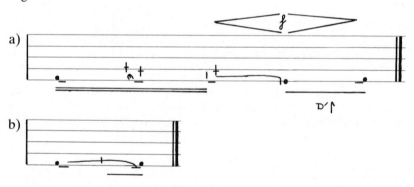

a) The 'van Manen walk', as analysed by the notator of his one-act work
   5 Tango's. The recording includes foot direction, ankle function, and
   dynamics.
b) The short form used throughout the score. A further value of the short
   form can be seen in this example: As the step takes place on one beat
   the analysis used throughout the score would place undue emphasis on
   the timing within one beat.
   In some modern dance works choreographers allow a certain
   amount of freedom for the dancers to develop their own variations

around a given idea or theme, in much the same way as contemporary composers allow freedom to instrumentalists within the body of a musical work. On some occasions it has been necessary for the notator to record all the variations developed by the dancers as a guide to subsequent performers. In other recording circumstances, instead of recording all the variations it has been preferable to record generalized instructions using 'dotted' information.

Fig. 195

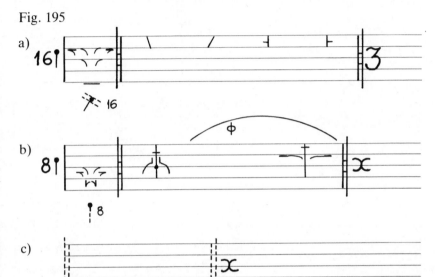

a) Sixteen dancers lying prone or supine facing the same direction, the head movement pattern being performed four times.
b) Eight dancers sitting facing any direction, the contraction and release movements being repeated as often as liked.
c) Rolling to the right for an unspecified number of times. Floor pattern and number of rolls unspecified.

   In recent years there has been a very strong cross-fertilization between the classical and modern dance forms in both schools and theatre. Classically based organizations offer their dancers classes in the modern technique and modern dance organizations employ an increasing number of dancers with classical dance training. This process is reflected in the content of choreographic scores as the languages of movement continually and increasingly blend.

Fig. 196

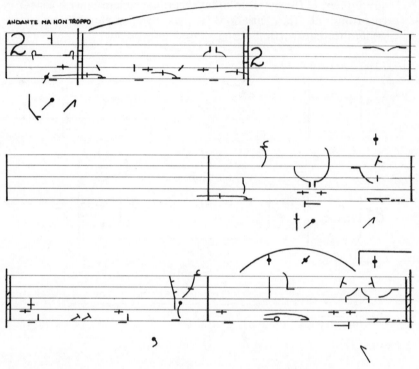

The opening bars from the 'Dance of the Sugar Plum Fairy' from *Nutcracker*, choreographed by Ivanov (1892).

Fig. 197

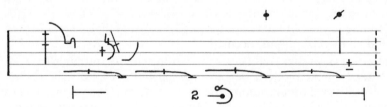

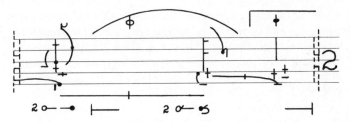

A section of London Contemporary Dance Theatre's *Step at a Time*, choreographed by Siobhan Davies (1976).

Fig. 198

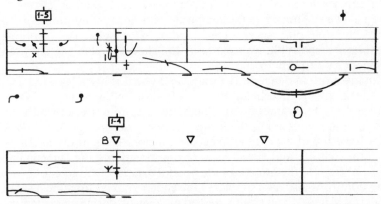

A section of Anastasia's 'Heartbeat' solo, from *Anastasia* Act III, choreographed by Kenneth MacMillan (1967), an example of the blending of two dance styles. In this excerpt the different structures of phrasing between the time signature of the music and the dancers' counts can be seen. While the music is written in bars of four, the dancers' counts change from a phrase of five to begin a phrase of four. See Chapter 10 for further reference to dancers' counts.

Writing the score

In drama and music the author is generally both the creator and the writer. In dance these two processes occur separately, though ideally they should take place at the same time, the notator writing the score as the choreographer creates the dances on the dancers.

The creative process varies from one choreographer to another, and in each case the notator must adjust the recording technique to suit the specific situation. Some choreographers have quite definite ideas when rehearsals commence and generally do not change them. In such cases the recording process is straightforward. However, quite the opposite is true of other choreographers, who develop their ideas on the dancers, creating movements which are directly influenced by the dancers' style and temperament. Gradually the final dance form is evolved by changing details from rehearsal to rehearsal and so the notator has to be prepared to keep altering the working score until the final dance structure is reached.

It is worth noting here that the recording of a dancer's interpretation of a role does not generally have a place in the choreographic score written for the preservation of a choreographic work. Just as a music score is written as the inspiration of the composer, allowing for interpretation, so is the choreographic score. The notator, working in the recording situation, is responsible for separating the choreographer's intent from the dancer's interpretation.

In many modern dance works sound and visual effects play a role in a way that is quite different to the role of music and lighting in classical works. Often the visual effects of lighting and props are set whilst the choreographer is creating the work. Notators in modern dance companies have found it possible to record precise details of the timing of important lighting and sound cues on the notation score, functioning somewhat beyond the bounds of the notator's initial involvement.

The notator is also able to release the choreographer from the need to memorize a newly created theme or movement during the intensive creative stage of choreography. Norman Morrice, director of the Royal Ballet, recalls: 'I have the habit of creating by moving spontaneously to the music, and it is often difficult for me (even immediately after the event) to analyse the movements. They may feel good and right when I am doing them, but I cannot tell exactly what I have done. Here the notator is invaluable: the observing eye that captures and records spontaneous movements which might otherwise be lost.'[1]

As rehearsals progress details become clearly defined and the score finally stands as the documentation of the choreographic idea. It is a complete record of the steps of each dancer, and the direction and whereabouts on the stage of each person, all this information being correlated with the music. Subsequently the score is completed with a variety of additional notes including analysis of steps where needed,

---

1 'Advantages of Benesh Notation to a Choreographer', N. Morrice, *Ballet Today* (January/February 1967).

production notes, stage plans and copyright information; in all a vast and comprehensive work. In a great number of cases a copy is sent to the Institute library in London, ensuring secure protection for the score, and registering it. The advent of a method of fixing the choreographic creation should be welcomed by all choreographers, as for copyright to exist in a work it must be recorded in a form suitable to the medium. The notation of dance works creates the best tangible recorded form of the creator's work. One of the difficulties of pursuing a case of infringement of choreographic copyright is in identifying the dance content. Through the written work it is possible for expert evidence to be presented in a court of law as the steps can be identified and the date that the work was made (e.g. through its registration with the library at the Institute of Choreology) provided.

Misunderstanding still exists with respect to the use of the video tape. In much the same way as records do not replace music scores in the musical arts, video tapes do not replace choreographic scores. Both have different functions in the preservation of dance works.

The video preserves the individual interpretation of the artist. The choreographic score preserves the choreographer's intention and records all necessary information in analysed (dissected) form, including the dancers' locations and entrances and exits. In video recordings of large dance works stage locations are easily obscured and it is often impossible to follow the movements of individuals. Such recordings do not present the movement content in dissected form. Furthermore, analysis from video recordings is often impeded by reduction of scale and image reversal.

Our dance heritage, which in the past has come near to being threatened with extinction, is now being protected in dance company libraries throughout the world. Perhaps the most striking example of the Notation preserving the works of a contemporary choreographer is in the case of John Cranko, whose untimely death in 1973 left a vacuum in the dance world. Most of his great dance works are recorded in BMN, thus securing them for the future and ensuring that they are reproduced authentically and with the Cranko style. Horst Koegler, the eminent German dance critic, after viewing the restaging at Munich of Cranko's *Taming of the Shrew*, commented that no one could doubt that it could be mounted by another company from the notation score. He added that the Munich *Shrew* was a first-class theatrical event, and as such a brilliant justification of BMN.[1]

1 'Glanzendes Cranko-Remake', Horst Koegler, *Suddeutsche Zeitung* (April 1976).

10. The Score in Use

BMN in the dance training timetable

Students fortunate enough to train in schools attached to ballet companies study the company repertoire as part of their training. In schools where the Notation is taught they have the added advantage of studying their repertoire classes through the written score. The Notation teacher with the Australian Ballet School, which is attached to the Australian Ballet Company, notes: 'Notation is also incorporated into other classes such as Solo Repertoire in which the students work on their technique, having first learnt the solos from the Notation score. They also notate their classical examination studies, under supervision, before each yearly examination. As well as being good recording practice, this helps their performance of the enchaînements. Having had to analyse them, they perform the dances with better attention to detail and better understanding of the music.'[1]

In 1978 at the annual performance of the Royal Ballet School students, the cast taught themselves their parts with the aid of the choreographic score. They learn the Notation as part of their dance training and in that year the 16–18-year-olds were to dance Ashton's *Birthday Offering* and MacMillan's *Diversions*. Each attended rehearsals with their score, and consequently when typical questions arose, such as 'which way do I turn?' or 'which hand is in front?', instead of asking the notator or ballet mistress the dancers referred to the Notation. When score reading has become an everyday subject in the lives of all dancers this will become commonplace in the rehearsal room.

Dance technique syllabuses

As a particular approach to teaching dance evolves and becomes recognized as a specific style of dancing, academies and societies are founded to teach and examine the system. It then becomes necessary to commit to

1 'The Australian Ballet School', Cherie Trevaskis, *The Choreologist*, No. 8. IOC publication (December 1975).

paper the nuances of the style. Hitherto, students and teachers have only been able to keep longhand notes. With this process some imperative information is inevitably lost. But now, as an increasing number of syllabuses are notated, the fine details of the technique are clearly described and communicated. To date the R.A.D. grades, the elementary, intermediate, and advanced I.S.T.D. National dance syllabus and the Bournonville classes have all been published in BMN. The Cechetti grades and advanced syllabuses are notated, and Madame Cleo Nordi's teachings based on the classes of Nicholas Legat are in the process of being recorded.

Fig. 199

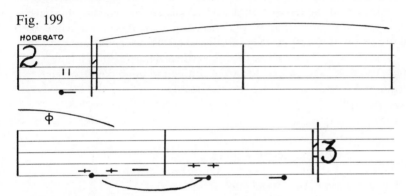

Grand Plié with changement from the Tuesday class of the Bournonville class syllabus.[1]

Fig. 200

1   *The Bournonville classes in BMN*, S. Caverely (Marcel Dekker, 1979).

A Glissades exercise from the R.A.D. Children's Examination Syllabus, Girls' Grade III.[1]

Composition and analysis

Composers learn their technique of composition partly by making a detailed analysis of the standard works available. In the training of dancers both the study of dance works and the subject of composition have been almost completely ignored. However, with the increasing number of both contemporary works and the surviving classics secured in written form, students can now analyse dance works in depth, thus raising their degree of understanding of dance structures. It is now possible, with the precision of notation, to assess dance forms in specific terms.

Some principal structures through which dance can be analysed are listed; the first two, 1a and 1b, are examined in some detail through two solos and a section of a dance for two people.

In solo work:

1   Motifs: a) balance
            b) use of repetition
            c) development of themes
2   Analysis of stage areas used and directions faced
3   Relationship between the dance and music

In group work:

1   Motifs: a) balance
            b) use of repetition
            c) development of themes
            d) use of repetition between dancers, e.g. as a canon
2   Balance of groups on the stage
3   Relationship between the dance and music

Vera Krassovskaya, currently Professor of Dance at the Theatre Science Faculty of the Leningrad Theatre Institute, delightfully describes Petipa's 5th variation (Violente), often called the Finger Variation, from the Prologue to *The Sleeping Beauty*: 'The dance was constructed of a sharp alternation of runs and an impetuous, actually "dishevelled" chain of movements. Here the choreographer specified completely unclassical positions of the arms; tense with fingers stretched out and pointed, they

---

1   *RAD Children's examination syllabus for girls and boys*, J. Jones (RAD, 1982).

cut through the air like flashing lightning. The entire variation has the
suddenness of a short thunderstorm.'[1] The dance as viewed by the
audience may seem dishevelled, but detailed examination of the score
reveals a coherent balanced structure. The dance consists of two distinct
sections, the first of 41 bars and the second of 31 bars. Each section is
carefully choreographed as an individual unit and comparison of the two
sections reveals a subtle difference of construction, the whole presenting
an ingenious dance full of impact.

Fig. 201   (pages 107–110)

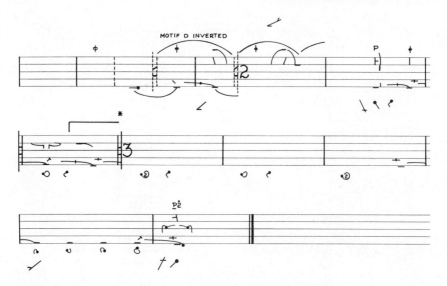

Balance

An overall analysis shows that the dance contains six motifs, these clearly dividing it into two separate sections:

9 bars	Introduction	
8 bars	motif A	
8 bars	motif B	
8 bars	motif C	section one
8 bars	motif A inverted	
7 bars	motif D	
4 bars	motif E	
12 bars	motif F	section two
7 bars	motif D inverted	
1 bar	finishing position	

Motifs A and D with their respective inversions are discussed below.

Within the first section, the structure is simple and symmetrical. Beginning and ending this section, the A motif and its inversion are also simple and symmetrical without decoration or development. Although the dancer moves around the stage in motifs B and C, Petipa returns her to the same stage location by the beginning of the inversion of motif A. Similarly the motif and its inversion do not move off the location.

Section one

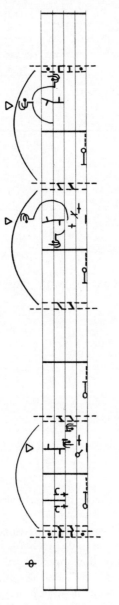

Motif A   bars 10–17

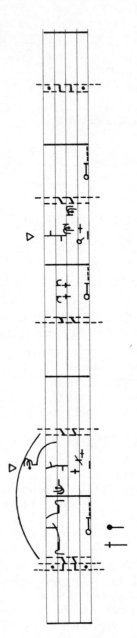

Motif A Inverted   bars 34–41

Section two

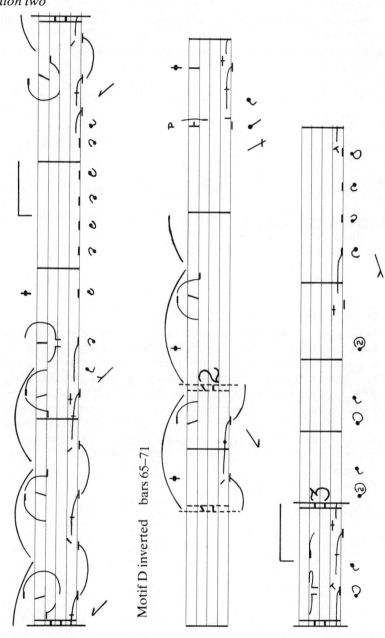

Motif D   bars 42–48

Motif D inverted   bars 65–71

Unlike the simple structure of section one, the structure of section two is more complex. This reflects clearly in analysis of the above-quoted motifs and in the lengths of motifs E and F. Whereas motif A and its inversion use a simple dance pattern and a simple stage location, the D motif inversion exists in the dancer's use of the stage.

Motif D 〵 followed by 〵 followed by 〵 (direction faced is 〵)

Motif D
inversion ⁄ followed by ⁄ followed by final position in bar 72

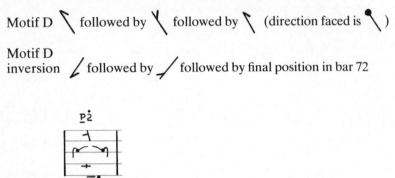

Use of Repetition

Repetition can be seen in many aspects of dance structures such as dynamics, floor patterns, repetition of movement, etc. It is a two-edged technique. On the one hand by repeating an enchaînement the audience has the opportunity to become familiar with the dance pattern. On the other hand repetition can become boring. The skill of the choreographer is to find the balance. When using repetition one technique is to perform the motif three times, completing the sequence with a short coda which is often related in some way to the main pattern. This use of repetition is analysed in the following section of the Girl's Solo in the Blue Bird variation from *The Sleeping Beauty*, Act III.

Fig. 202

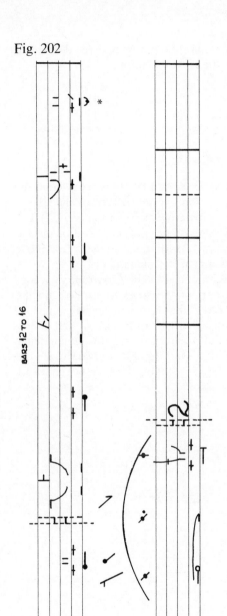

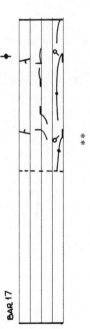

* Hopping; see Chapter 11 for recording hopping.
** Diagonal steps backwards. Diagonal movement has not been described in this book.

The theme is performed three times, but the pas de bourrée derrière at the end of the last repeat indicates the end of the motif.

Fig. 203   Bar 18

The simple new motif established at the end of bar 17 is repeated in the bar 18 coda, bringing to completion the overall pattern of the six-bar sequence. Two important relationships are echoed in the coda: i) The head, tilted and turned from side to side echoes the head position used at the beginning and during the main motif; and ii) the diagonal retirés move backwards echoing the hops backwards of the main theme.

A further use of the repetition technique gives the opportunity to move the dancer or dancers from one part of the stage to another. In the following example from *Swan Lake* the four-bar enchaînement is performed seven times in all, covering 28 bars of music. At first glance one may be forgiven for thinking that the repetition leads the audience into a state of boredom. However, this is not the case, as Ivanov uses the steps to cover various areas of the stage thus giving the audience changing views of the same movements.

Fig. 204   Tempo di Valse

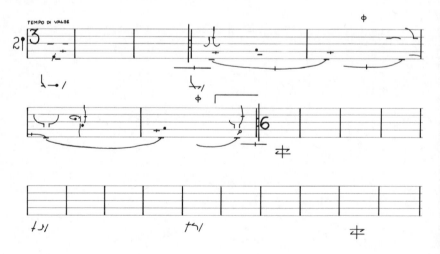

The opening section, Dance of the Leading Swans from Act II of *Swan Lake*. Note the dash after the travelling sign, indicating that the other dancer is performing the same steps, whilst reflecting the stage pattern.

The following stage diagrams with the travelling signs show the stage patterns danced by the Leading Swans.

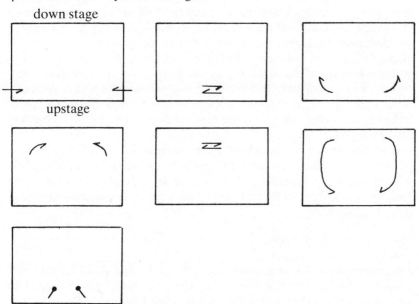

Rehearsing from the score

Arguably the most important current use of the choreographic score is in company rehearsals. The notator is called upon to use the scores under a number of different circumstances. Dancers frequently are required to adopt a system of counting which matches the dynamics or repetition of the dance movements, rather than the time signature of the music. Both the dancers' counts and the music counts are linked in the body of the choreographic score. During rehearsals the dancers work to piano accompaniment which necessarily reduces many complexities found in the full orchestral score. When rehearsals progress to full orchestral accompaniment any underlying conflict between the two counting structures is greatly reduced by reference to the choreographic score.

Frequently when a ballet has been out of the repertoire for some time there is a need both to refresh the memory of those dancers who were previously involved, and to teach sections to new dancers who have since joined the company. Also, urgent rehearsals may be called when a dancer is injured or taken ill and an understudy is needed. The notator can be called to take these rehearsals which require the part to be learnt in a very short time.

Notators not only work from scores which they have written: A company, when choosing to present a work which has not previously been in its repertoire but has been recorded elsewhere, can acquire a copy of the dance score so that the resident notator can mount the work. Such arrangements are only made with the permission of the choreographer and the owner or commissioner of the work. On the other hand some choreographers, who have a close working relationship with a particular notator, will prefer to send that notator with the score to mount the work. In both cases the choreographer may then, but not always, attend the final rehearsals to add the 'finishing touches' to the production.

Kathrine Sorley Walker observed such a reconstruction from a choreographic score. She wrote that it is certainly a justification for a notation system when the Australian Ballet can be seen dancing a version of *La Fille mal gardée* faithfully reproduced from the choreographic score sent from England.[1]

Fig. 205   (pages 117–18)

An excerpt from Lise's Ribbon Dance from the first act of *La Fille mal gardée* by Sir Frederick Ashton. Note the supporting signs on the hands indicating the hands holding the ribbon. (See Chapter 11 for recording supporting objects.)

1   Dance and Its Creators, K. S. Walker (The John Day Co., New York, 1972).

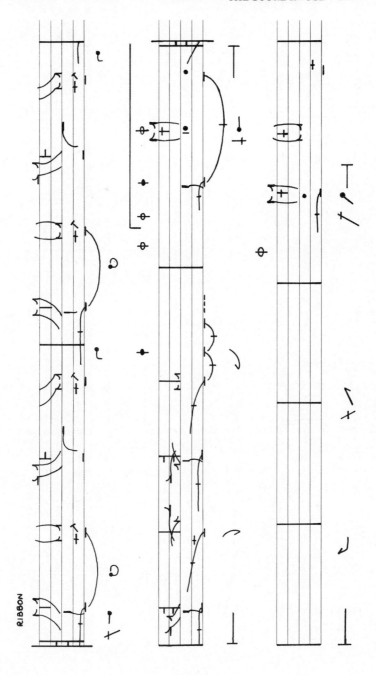

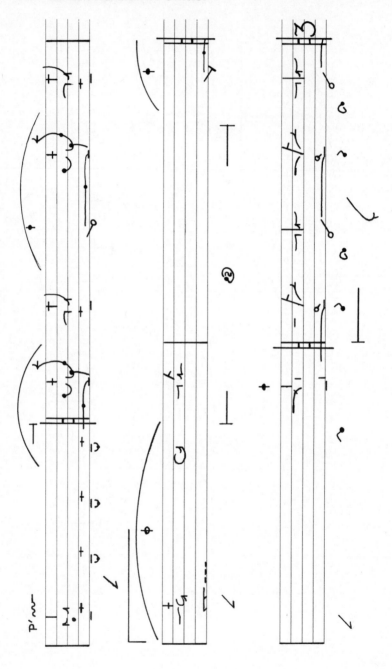

Another example occurred with *Four Schumann Pieces*, when the same work was mounted in two companies simultaneously. The Dutch choreographer Hans van Manen created the one-act work for the Royal Ballet in London in 1975. During rehearsals the work was recorded in BMN, this being the normal procedure to preserve the repertoire of this great company. Following the success of the production the National Ballet of Canada requested the ballet for its repertoire. It was therefore arranged for a notator from the Royal Ballet to mount the work in Toronto from the choreographic score. Meanwhile, the choreographer was staging it in Amsterdam for the Dutch National Ballet, and in the process rechoreographing sections. The resident notator with the Amsterdam company recorded the freshly created alterations and sent them to the notator in Canada. This ensured that the Canadian production was the revised version. This revision would have been impossible by 'word of mouth'. Furthermore it would have been impractical and expensive for an individual to travel between the two companies with the information.

In some cases the company choreologist has found the time to teach the Notation to interested dancers. As a result they can prepare themselves for a new role, thus cutting down on rehearsal time. This 'by-product' of the work of the company choreologist points the way to the future. As more and more dancers learn the Notation they will learn their roles logically and speedily in private. When an entire company is able to do this, rehearsal time, which is extremely expensive, will be dramatically cut. Dame Ninette de Valois, founder of the Royal Ballet, points out in *Step by Step* that 'everyone learns to read and write, and a dancer must eventually be able to read movement as the basis of his general dance education . . . we visualise a day when a young artist will be capable of putting in some private study, through notation reading, of the many roles to be learnt in a big repertory company.'[1]

1 Step by Step, N. de Valois (W. H. Allen, 1977).

11. Further Dance

Historical dance

In the Western world music, painting, architecture, and literature all have their past achievements available for understanding and study in permanent form. Thus their place in history can be clearly understood. Dance however is the poor relation, simply because concrete evidence of dances from the past does not exist, as a complete dance notation was not available to preserve them.

In the last fifty years or so a growing number of dedicated researchers have studied the available evidence, mainly manuscripts, and to a degree the history of dance can now be understood. However, an element of conjecture is always present. Dances reconstructed from historical sources, are thought of as historical dances, distinguishing them from folk dances which in the past have been handed down via the oral tradition. One of the most valuable sources of descriptions of 16th-century dance is the *Orchésographie* published in 1588.[1] It was written by Thoinot Arbeau, Canon of Langres, who was a scholar and churchman. Postures and steps of dances of the period are described in detail, then their names abbreviated to the first letter, e.g. the steps 'single' and 'double' are notated respectively as s and d. These letters were then placed by the correct musical notes.

Fig. 206   (p. 121)

A Pavane, danced to the tune 'Belle qui tiens ma vie'. It is notated in the *Orchésographie* as ssd ss d ss d ss d. The information = written in the lower stave indicates that the steps recorded in the upper stave are also executed by ♀. These signs are described in repeat signs.

---

1   *Orchésographie*, Thoinot Arbeau, translated by Mary Stewart Evans (Dover Pub. Inc., New York, 1967).

demi = quarter throughout

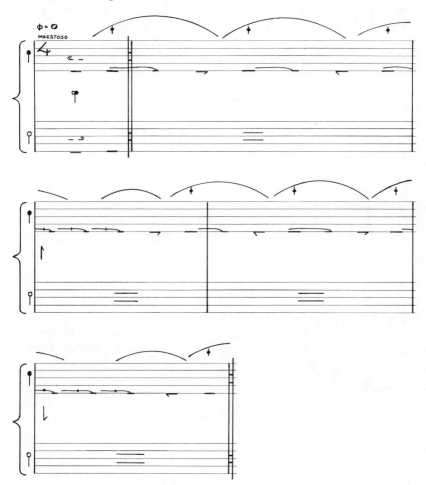

Baroque dance has been mainly researched from publications
recording dances in Feuillet notation. Although it is generally accepted
that Pierre Beauchamps (dancing master and choreographer to Louis
XIV) invented the system, it is popularly known as Feuillet notation.
Chorégraphie, ou l'Art de Dé'crire la Dance was published in 1700 by the
dancer and choreographer Raoul Auger Feuillet.[1] The notation

1 *Chorégraphie, ou l'Art de Dé'crire la Dance* (Paris, 2nd edition, 1701).

recorded the floor plan of the dances with paths of movement for each dancer mapped out with a line. Along this line the symbols for foot positions were placed, linked by step lines showing movement forwards, backwards and sideways. On to the step lines and foot positions were placed signs for plier, relever, glisser, and sauter. All movements become combinations of these signs.

   Feuillet notation of the step – 'to spring forwards, both feet joined'

   the same step backwards

Both theatrical and social dances were recorded in the notation, there being little difference in their techniques at the time. The system did not, however, record body movements. Consequently when the dance technique developed into a more complex form the notation fell out of use.

Fig. 207

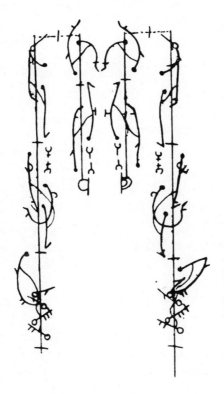

An extract from *La Mariée*, a pas de deux by M. Pécour, Composer of Ballets for the Royal Academy of Music, Paris, notated by Feuillet.

Fig. 208

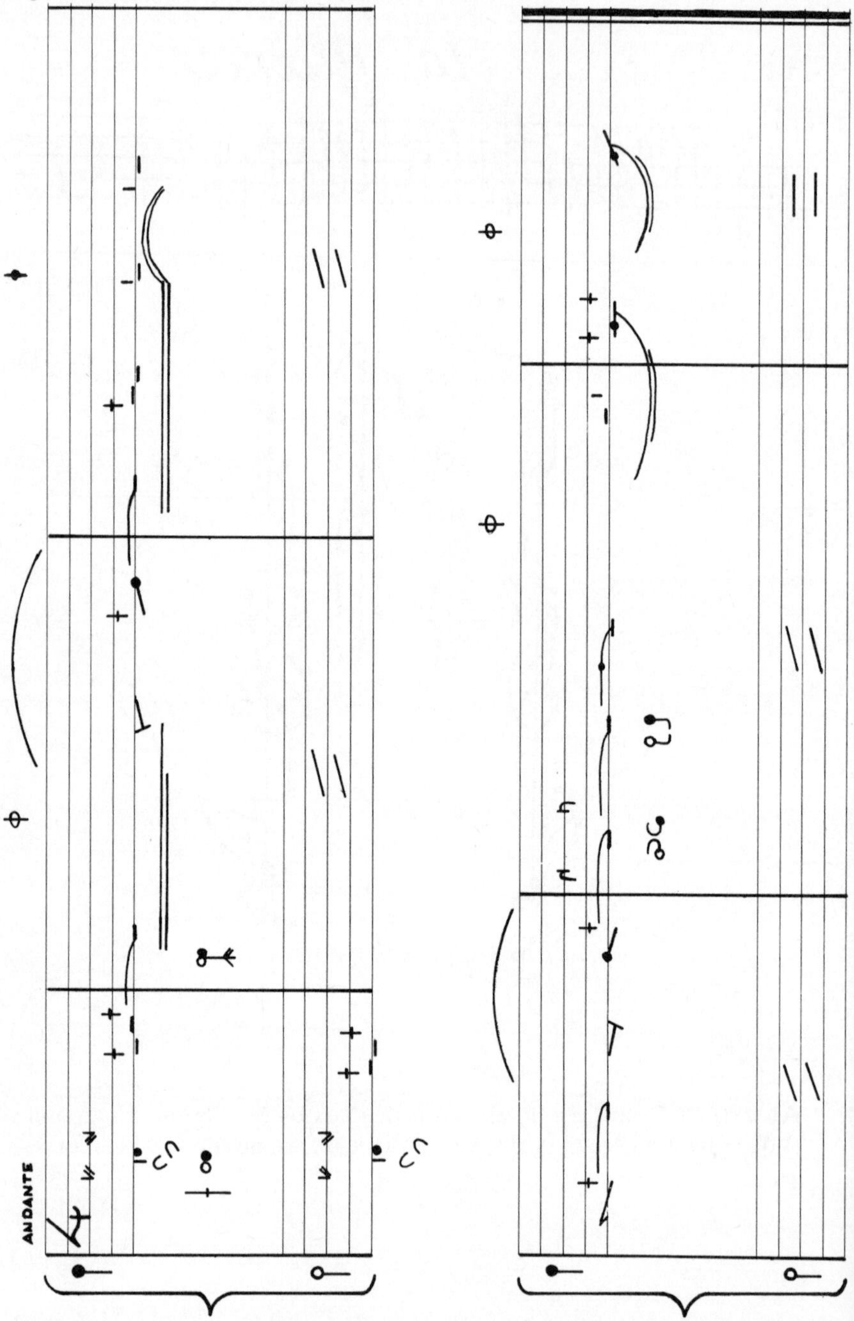

The same extract as Fig. 207, renotated in BMN. The information $\succ$ and = in the second stave indicates that ↑ executes the steps recorded in the upper stave, firstly 'on the other side', then 'on the same side'. Note the final two steps are skimming jumps.

Currently, a distinguished dance researcher is translating and describing two 18th-century European books of dance instruction and dances. To assist her in this difficult and slow task a notator works alongside her, recording in BMN each movement as it is clarified from the translation. This process ensures that each time the researcher leaves the work, she is able, upon returning to it, to have access to authoritative, accurate, detailed records.

Indian dance

In India, the transmission of dance without a notation has been achieved through the special relationship between the teacher – the guru – and pupil. Highly developed systems of teaching classical Indian dance have maintained the ancient traditions with great fidelity. But social changes in India now imperil important areas of its heritage. Changes in audiences, patrons and dancers, and changes in the relationship between gurus and pupils mean that the traditional system of preservation can no longer be relied on. The question of the use of movement notation is now topical.[1]

Bharata Natyam is a classical dance style which tells legends and stories through a highly complex series of movements, particularly hand gestures. In BMN these are simply analysed above the stave using the finger notation described in Chapter 8.

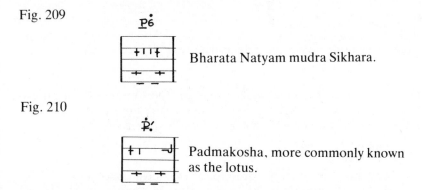

Fig. 209

Bharata Natyam mudra Sikhara.

Fig. 210

Padmakosha, more commonly known as the lotus.

1   'Notating Indian Dance', Sangeet Natak 9 *Journal of the Performing Arts*, New Delhi.

Fig. 211

A 'Bharata Natyam' backwards walk.

In Indian dance there are typical movements when the arms sweep through a wide arc. The body moves to enable these arm patterns to take place. The type of movement needed is understood within the movement language and is therefore not recorded.

Fig. 212

Whilst the arms are moving the body bends at the hip, then returns to the upright.

Fig. 213

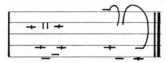

Upper torso side tilts as the right arm moves.

The above three examples make use of the short form of writing dorsiflexion at the ankle when the foot flexes upwards towards the shin. This action is recorded by modifying the extremity signs as follows:

On a forward sign ⬆

On a level sign ➖●➖

Lateral head movements are typical of Indian dance styles. These movements are not side tilts as described in Chapter 3, but lateral movements which displace the head from side to side without tilting.

Fig. 214

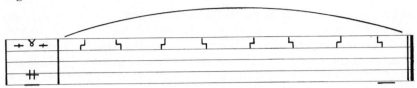

This sequence is from a dance of the Pahari people who live on the lower reaches of the Himalayas. The hands are together and in contact with the back of the head. The legato line links the knee extension and the foot movement smoothly over the time taken to execute the eight head movements.

Fig. 215

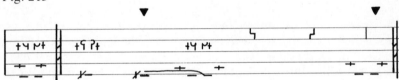

Section of a Kathakali Sari Dance. Note the audible accents over the relevant foot.

Fig. 216

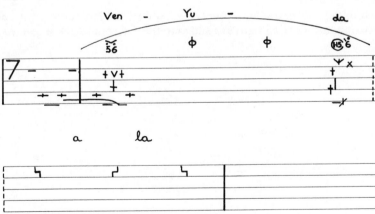

An excerpt from a Shabdam (song-dance). The words of the song are written above the stave.

National dance

The national or folk dances of countries mirror the mythology and customs of the past. In the majority of cases dances have been handed down from generation to generation by 'word of mouth'. To some the oral tradition is an essential aspect of folk dances in spite of the fact that with oral tradition alone dance forms can die. At the turn of the century the Morris dances of England were in danger of dying out as they were not being handed down from one generation to another. However, Cecil Sharp (collector and publisher of songs and dances of England) travelled to numerous English villages researching and recording folk dances in his limited notation system. He is credited with saving this national heritage, more than any other single person.

Fig. 217   (opposite)

The opening and A section of the Winster Morris Reel, performed by two files of eight dancers each. This dance is part of the June Ceremonial from Winster in Derbyshire. The dancers perform this processional dance whilst travelling through the town. The file of eight dancers on the right γ . , known as the Ladies Side (although it is always performed by men), wear hats decorated with flowers. The dancers hold handkerchiefs throughout this dance, recorded through the following theory.

Supporting objects
The holding of inanimate objects is known in Notation terms as supporting. Supporting signs are added to the extremity signs as follows:

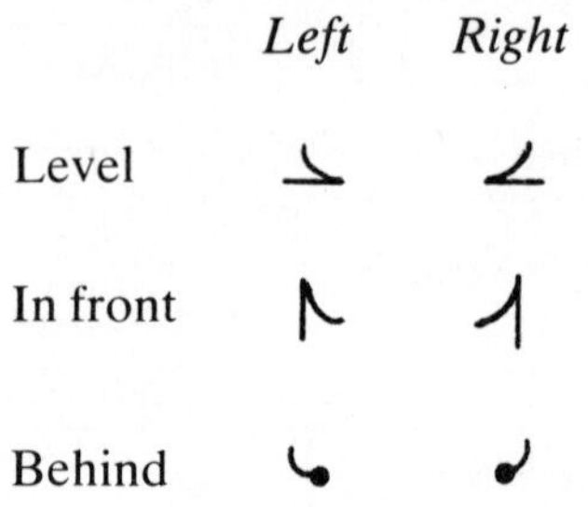

	Left	*Right*
Level	⌣	⌣
In front	⌐	⌐
Behind	⌣	⌣

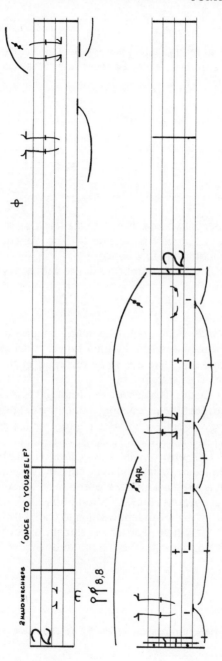

Hopping

A step common to many dances is hopping which can be executed on the spot (the most common form) or travelling. It is recorded with a contracted jump line.

Fig. 218

Hops occur on beats two and three. As the left leg does not move during the hops it is unnecessary to restate it. The clenched hands-on-waist position is typical of many folk dances.

'Oxen Gallop' is a lively humorous dance with heavy steps.

Fig. 219   (opposite)

This Austrian circle dance is for 'as many couples as will'. The information ⸔ previously described within repeat brackets is placed in the lower stave indicating that the steps recorded in the stave above are repeated 'on the other side' by ↑ .

The National Dance Branch of the Imperial Society of Teachers of Dancing exists to foster the teaching and enjoyment of national dances. An examination system, sub-divided into Elementary, Intermediate, Advanced Grades, and Medal Tests, ensures that standards are maintained. In 1976–7 the entire syllabus was notated with background notes. Joan Lawson, dance historian and national dance expert, wrote in *Dance*: 'the compilation is a remarkable achievement . . . there are copious notes on the history, geography, music, costume style and other details. In fact everything needed by the student wishing to take the major examinations of the branch . . . it will provide a most valuable record of the work of the National Dance Branch in furthering the study of folk dance . . .'[1]

1   *Dance. The Journal of the Imperial Society of Teachers of Dancing*, No. 14 (1977). Joan Lawson.

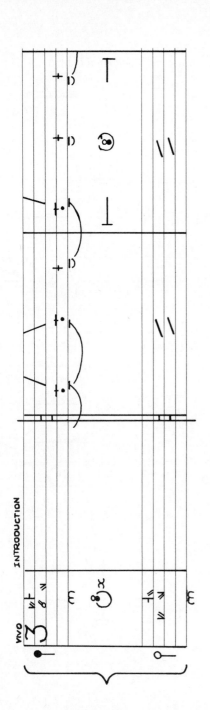

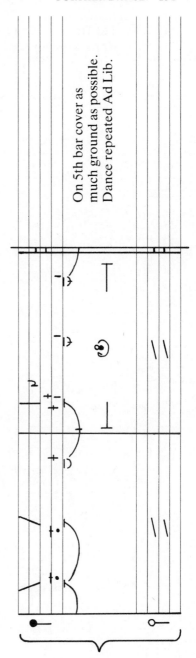

On 5th bar cover as much ground as possible. Dance repeated Ad Lib.

Fig. 220   The Breton Sabot dance from the ISID National Dance
Branch syllabus.

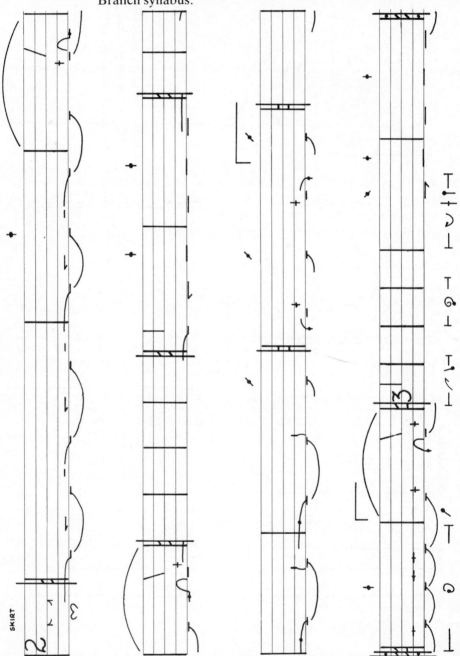

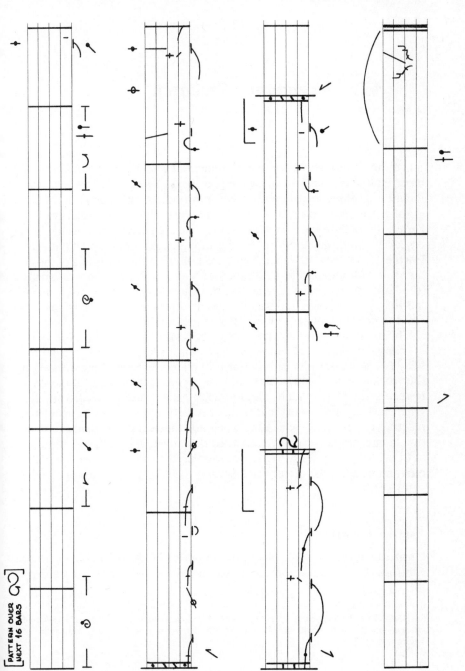

12. *Ergonomic Research*

Since the emergence of human movement as a field of research more and more machines have been developed to aid this study. However, the techniques these instruments have introduced, e.g. time-lapse photography and computer simulation, are invariably very expensive and generally analyse specific movements. Such machines are unsuitable in research situations requiring the recording of gross movement patterns. Furthermore they are laboratory-based, making the recording of movement *in situ* impossible. On the other hand, in P. A. Kember's words, 'the Notation can be used wherever recording and analysis of movements has to be carried out', and is capable of modification: 'it can be adapted to suit the needs of an individual research project.'[1]

The five-lined stave is capable of great flexibility, recording, as it were, in 'close-up'. It can be employed as a 'waist stave', recording from the head to the waist only. This has proved effective in recording workers at the work bench. Further 'close-up' usages are modifications of the stave to record the face or hands. Additionally it can be used to record objects. One such usage in work study has been to record a sewing machine, plotting the points at which the machinist touched it, whilst at the same time an accompanying stave recorded the movements of the operator.

In the following study two staves were used during the collection of the movement data; the upper stave became a chair stave, the lower one the sitter's stave.

Easy-chair comfort[2]

Until the research took place, the majority of studies into easy-chair comfort had been laboratory based. Since evidence increasingly

1 'The Benesh Movement Notation used to study sitting behaviour', P. Kember, *Applied Ergonomics* (July 1976).
2 *A preliminary field study of sitting comfort and easy chairs with a new observational method*, P. Kember, Professor B. Shackel, P. Branton, Loughborough University of Technology (1972).

suggested that subjects in the artificial setting of the laboratory behave differently from subjects in the natural setting, it was felt important to be able to describe the sitting behaviour of easy-chair users under normal conditions. The analysis of the movement data collected during this research clearly established that the sitters were indeed influenced by their surroundings and other people.

Thus the primary aim of the research was to collect movement data of easy-chair users *in situ*. The secondary aim was to ensure that the data should be so presented that it could assist in the improvement of easy chairs design.

The study required a recording technique other than cameras, as permission had been obtained to carry out the work in a hotel lobby providing cameras were not used. It further required that the recording technique had to be capable of recording as fast as the behaviour was occurring. Following a preliminary study BMN was shown to be capable of these requirements. Two approaches to the movement data were presented for analysis and classification:

i) Identifying postures, or parts of postures, common to all or some of the subjects.

ii) Examining each subject to glean an understanding of the behaviour of that particular individual.

Both approaches were possible using the Notation.

Environmental measurements were also noted. These included noise level (which sometimes effected whether the sitter leaned forwards in the chair), lighting levels, humidity and temperature, chair dimensions, 'hardness' of chair, cushioning and fabric, and the sitters' clothing.

The chair stave

Fig. 221

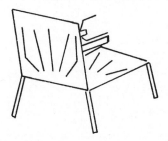

The chair was viewed from behind with the following location signs

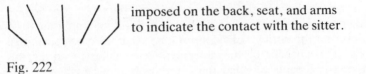 imposed on the back, seat, and arms to indicate the contact with the sitter.

Fig. 222

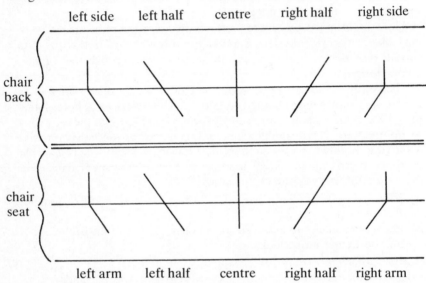

The signs imposed on the stave. The double line indicates the point where the chair back and seat meet.

Flexed joints supported

In many instances the sitters' flexed elbows rested on the chair arms. The flexed joint signs are modified with supported signs to record flexed joints supported on inanimate objects.

Fig. 223

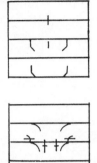

Torso in contact with chair back at two points; showing these two significant points of contact conditions the contact of the remainder of the body. The arm rests are supporting the arms at two points (1) the elbows (2) the hands. The support signs indicate that the hips and shoulders are supported. Note that no hands are recorded. They are, in fact, masked directly in front of the elbows, resting on chair arms; their position is quite specific.

Fig. 224

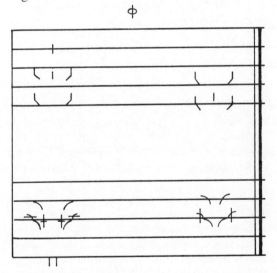

The subject moves into a slumped position by sliding the buttocks forwards in the chair. Note the changing points of contact in the chair stave, the support signs moving up to the upper shoulder areas and the supported elbows changing position, from ⊰ ⊱ (supported level with the body) to ⊀ ⊁ (supported in front of the body).

The two frames below are from a recording of a woman wearing trousers and a jumper. It was noted that this clothing gave her considerable freedom of movement.

Fig. 225

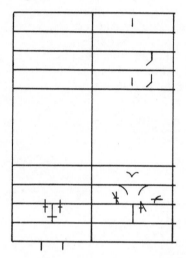

The first frame (extracted from a complete recording) shows her sitting with legs apart and bending forwards at the hips. She then sat up till her upper back and head were supported by the chair. Additionally she flexed the left leg and placed the left foot on the right flexed knee.

Reliability and validity of Benesh Movement Notation

The authors of this research carried out a reliability test on BMN using sitting behaviour data. Initially, a 15-minute video tape, using two cameras, was made. The postures of an easy-chair sitter included as wide a range of activity as possible. Five notators recorded the video on five separate occasions.

The first testing was to have the results analysed by another notator. She noted each movement of the head, trunk, arms, hips, and legs against a time scale. When this test was again repeated by the same notator one month later, the results of test one completely agreed with the results of test two. The results of this test were submitted to computer analysis and supported the validity of BMN as an accurate recording system.

A further test involved a random selection of postures from the video being 'acted out' by a subject. Once in position the sitter was photographed from two angles (the same angles as filmed by the two cameras). This was repeated using the recordings made by each of the notators during the previous test. The photographs, when compared, again supported the validity of BMN.

A Brief History of Benesh Movement Notation

It was in 1947 that Rudolf and Joan Benesh first considered the problems of devising a practical and efficient notation system. Joan was a dancer and Rudolf an accountant with a deep interest in scientific subjects as well as being an artist, having trained at the Wimbledon College of Art. The concept of a notation was fired by Joan's attempts at recording her ideas for a ballet she wished to create. Rudolf quickly set his mind to the problem, directly and indirectly drawing on concepts of music, per-spective drawing, linguistics, and the new scientific disciplines of ergonomics, information theory, and cybernetics.[1]

Like many of history's greatest inventions the basic concepts came almost as a flash of inspiration. For Rudolf there was no lengthy period of research, though there can be no doubt that his years of logical appli-cation to numbers as an accountant, and his training as an artist in observing the human body, had laid the foundation for the thought processes required to structure a universal notation system. He appreci-ated in a very short time the problems involved. Although the concepts were simple, the detailed workings were initially complicated and it took many years of work to refine and simplify the Notation into a streamlined system.

No sooner had the Beneshes established the basic Notation elements than they realized the signs were in fact 'an alphabet' which could record the vast and complicated phenomenon of *all* forms of movement. These signs in isolation could not function as a notation of creative thought, just as the letters of the written alphabet do not in themselves convey or preserve ideas and words. It is only when the alphabet is constructed in an orderly manner into words, and these words are constrained in their use by the rules of syntax and grammar, that language evolves to become a creative tool of communication and thought. The Beneshes realized the same was true of the Notation signs and their construction into movement languages. It is only when the signs are placed on the Notation stave, and regulated by the rules of syntax and grammar, that they communicate movement data. For those readers interested in the development of

1   *Reading Dance*, R. and J. Benesh (Souvenir Press (E&S) Ltd, 1977).

languages in movement, Rudolf Benesh's writings have been published in *Theoria to Theory*.[1]

The contribution of Rudolf Benesh's invention to the vast and varied world of movement studies is freely acknowledged by experts in many different fields of movement. What sort of man was he, the mind that dominated the Notation and the Institute of Choreology until his tragic and unexpected death in 1975? He was a quiet introspective person, hiding a delightful sense of humour, his mind ranging widely over a vast area of scientific subjects, music and painting. He gave the appearance of being somewhat remote, preferring small gatherings to large public appearances. It is therefore not surprising that it was in the privacy of Institute staff meetings or tutorials that the brilliant workings of his mind could best be seen in action. When presented at such meetings with a Notation problem, he was immediately able to grasp the essential elements of both the problem and its solution in terms of the specific Notation point, and at the same time recognize the solution in terms of the Notation as a whole. This width of vision was the strength which produced a Notation that remains logical and consistent in all movement languages.

Although Benesh Movement Notation is applicable to all forms of movement it was as a movement notation in dance that it was first applied. By the time the Notation was fundamentally complete and had been tested on a small scale Joan Benesh was dancing with the Sadler's Wells Ballet (now the Royal Ballet), and in May 1955 Dame Ninette de Valois asked her to record John Cranko's ballet *The Lady and the Fool*.

The news of the invention spread, lectures and demonstrations were given and individuals commenced private training to learn the skill of notating. Further notators were trained through a correspondence course and through classroom teaching at the Sadler's Wells Ballet School. The Royal Ballet Company employed its first full-time Benesh notator in 1960, other companies all over the world following suit. As more and more people were trained it became inevitable that an examination system was required to maintain standards. And as the demand for notators grew it was increasingly urgent that a central body be founded to foster and co-ordinate the developments and application of the Notation. Thus the Institute of Choreology was founded, being registered as a charity in 1962. In 1965, with a joint grant from the Gulbenkian Foundation, the Pilgrim Trust, and the Leverhulme Trust the Institute headquarters and library were established. The premises were officially

1 *Birth of a Language*, R. Benesh, *Theoria to Theory*, Vol II (Gordon and Breach Science Publishers Ltd, 1978).

opened by Jennie Lee, then Minister of State with special responsibility for the arts. Rudolf Benesh became Director of the Institute and Joan Benesh Principal of the Training Course.

Through the world-wide use of the Notation, libraries of movement scores have been established for study and research purposes. However, the Institute houses the unique central library containing hundreds of movement scores. These include: Teaching syllabuses for the various Notation courses, research files in neurology, anthropology, and ergonomics, observations in non-verbal communication, computer research, traditional folk dance, Indian classical dance; dance syllabuses, classical ballets, contemporary dance works, and historical dances. There is also a large collection of relevant books. The Institute is a member of the British Copyright Council and is a central registration body for dance scores, enabling choreographers to protect, through copyright, their creations. Full-time courses are offered to train notators to the very high standards required in the professional world. Introductory and correspondence courses are also available.

The following are the principal events in the development of Benesh Movement Notation:

1947–1955   The evolution and completion of the Notation.
1955   Adopted by Sadler's Wells Ballet (now the Royal Ballet).
1956   *An Introduction to Benesh Dance Notation* published by A. and C. Black Limited.
1958   Benesh Movement Notation included amongst the scientific and technological developments in the British Government pavilion at the Brussels Universal Exposition.
1959   The first application of the Notation to work-study in collaboration with the Centre of Technological Studies for the Clothing Industry, Paris.
1960   First full-time notator employed by Royal Ballet.
1962   The Institute of Choreology founded.
1964   Grants from Gulbenkian Foundation and the Pilgrim and Leverhulme Trust enable permanent premises to be purchased at Barons Court, London.
1965   First full-time training course for notators.
1966   First use of the Notation by the medical profession at the Centro di Educazione Motoria, Florence.
1967   Arts Council of Great Britain provides annual grant. First application to educational needs in collaboration with Chelsea College and the publication by Max Parrish of *An*

Introduction to Benesh Movement Notation; Its general principles and its use in Physical Education.

1968   The first use of the Notation in anthropological research by the Australian Institute of Aboriginal Studies, the Australian Council for the Arts, and Monash University.

1969   Revised and extended edition of *An Introduction to Benesh Dance Notation* retitled *An Introduction to Benesh Movement Notation: Dance.*

1974   Founding of *The Choreologist*, the official Journal of the Institute.

1975   Rudolf Benesh dies.

1976   Joan Benesh retires from the Institute, remaining as consultant. Monica Parker, head of the Notation department of the Royal Ballet, becomes principal of the Institute and later director.

1978   First full-time Clinicians' Course as IOC. New multi-disciplinary correspondence course published, catering for all students of movement, whether they are physiotherapists, occupational therapists, modern dancers, classical dancers, computer programmers, anthropologists, or ergonomists. The publication of sheet-notation; the first edition being 'Grand Pas de Deux' from Act III of *The Sleeping Beauty*. The inaugural copy was presented to Dame Ninette de Valois on her eightieth birthday.
First section of the *Encyclopaedia of BMN*, 'The Stave', published by the IOC.

1979   First full-time Clinicians' Course taught outside the IOC at Queen's Medical Centre, Nottingham, funded by the South Nottingham District Health Authority with a part grant from the Trent Regional District.

1980   Lecture on BMN and its uses given to the All China Dancers Association, Peking.

1981   Short Introductory course in BMN given to staff of the Shanghai Ballet Company.

1981   Notation incorporated into new University of London 'O' Level Dance Syllabus.

1982   First International Summer School in BMN held at, and in co-operation with, The University of Waterloo, Canada. First Clinicians' Course (including the sitting of IOC Examinations) taught by qualified hospital personnel. Course attenders are staff of the South Nottingham District Physiotherapy Service.

Organizations with direct teaching or research links with the Institute of Choreology:
American Ballet Theatre School, New York
Arts Education Schools, London and Tring
Ashford Hospital, Surrey
Australian Ballet School
Australian Institute of Aboriginal Studies
Ballettschule der Hamburgischen Staatsoper
Bellairs School of Dance and Drama, Guildford
Bush Davies School, East Grinstead
Cambridge School of Physiotherapy
Cheyne Walk Centre for Spastic Children, London
Community Medicine Department, Guy's Hospital, London
Conservatorio Nacional, Lisbon
Dance Notation Bureau, New York
George Brown, The City College, Toronto
Izmir State Conservatory, Turkey
John Cranko Ballet School, Stuttgart
Lanchester Polytechnic Coventry, School of Physiotherapy
Legat School, Crowborough
London Studio Centre
Loughborough University of Technology
Mansfield General Hospital, Nottingham
Murilova Ballet School, Bournemouth
Newcomen Centre, Guy's Hospital, London
Normanby College, School of Physiotherapy, King's College Hospital, London
Pretoria Technicon
Queen's College Glasgow, School of Physiotherapy
Queen's Medical Centre, Nottingham
Queen's University, Belfast
Rambert School of Ballet, London
Royal Academy of Dancing, London
Royal Ballet Schools, London
Royal Swedish Ballet School
Southmead Hospital, Bristol
Stella Mann School of Dance, London
Ulster Polytechnic, Belfast, School of Physiotherapy
United States International University, San Diego
University of Izmir-Ege, Turkey
University of Queensland
University of Waterloo, Ontario

Victorian College of the Arts, Melbourne
Western Australia Academy of Performing Arts, Perth
Westminster City Hospital, London
York University, Toronto

Dance companies with full-time BMN notators. Numbers in brackets indicate more than one notator on the staff.

American Ballet Theatre (2)
Australian Ballet
Ballett der Bayerischen Staatsoper, Munich (2)
Ballet Rambert, London
Bat-Dor Dance Company, Tel-Aviv
CAPAB Ballet, Cape Town (2)
Covent Garden Royal Ballet, London (4)
Den Norske Opera, Oslo
Devlet Opera ve Balesi, Ankara
Devlet Opera ve Balesi, Istanbul
Hamburgische Staatsoper
Het Nationale Ballet, Amsterdam
London Festival Ballet (2)
National Ballet of Canada
New Zealand Ballet
PACT Ballet, Pretoria
Royal Swedish Ballet
Sadler's Wells Royal Ballet, London (2)
Scottish Ballet, Glasgow
Stuttgart Ballet
West Australian Ballet Company

N.B. Companies who frequently employ freelance BMN notators have not been listed.

Further Reading

Benesh Movement Notation – Beginners' Manual 1. 'Still-life.' Janet Wilks (Institute of Choreology, London, 1978).
Benesh Movement Notation – Beginners' Manual 2. 'Moving,' Janet Wilks (Institute of Choreology, London, 1980).
Benesh Movement Notation – An Introduction to recording clinical data. Julia McGuinness-Scott (Chartered Society of Physiotherapy pbn., London, 1982).
Birth of a Language. Rudolf Benesh (Institute of Choreology, 1970).
'Dance Notation and Aboriginal Culture' by Babette Morse, *Hemisphere* (November 1968).
'The Institute of Choreology' by Nicholas Dromgoole, *About the House –the Journal of Covent Garden* (Summer 1979).
'Linguistic Structures in Classical Ballet' by Kathleen Russell, *Theoria to Theory* (Gordon and Breach Science Publishers Ltd., 1977, Vol. II).
'My Work as a Choreologist with the Royal Ballet' by Faith Worth, *The Dancing Times* (June 1967).
'The Use of Benesh Notation in the Royal Ballet: John Field talking to Fernau Hall', *The Dancing Times* (August 1968).
'Writing Down the Rambert Repertoire' by Ann Whitley, *The Dancing Times* (July 1968).
A selection of dance reading material including excerpts from classical ballets and national dances is available from the Institute of Choreology.

Index